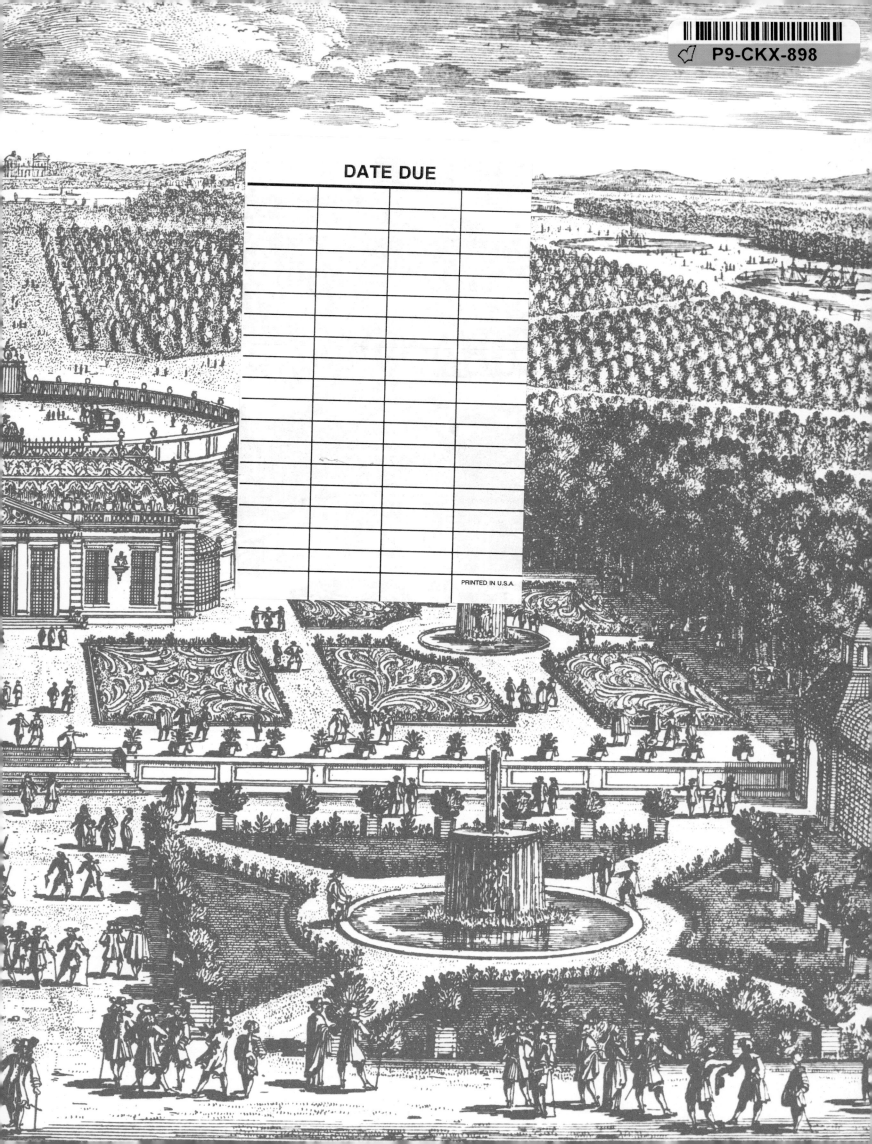

DATE DUE

P9-CKX-898

Great Palaces

Great Palaces

Introduction by Sacheverell Sitwell

Spring Books   London · New York · Sydney · Toronto

Originally published 1964 and © 1964 by
George Weidenfeld and Nicolson Limited, London

This edition published 1969 by
The Hamlyn Publishing Group Limited
London · New York · Sydney · Toronto
Hamlyn House, Feltham, Middlesex, England

Printed in Italy by
Arnoldo Mondadori Editore Officine Grafiche, Verona
SBN 600 01682 X

Contents

Introduction

Schönbrunn, Vienna, from across the parterre

THAT THE WORD 'PALACE' IS NO more synonymous with comfort than 'great' is indicative of aesthetic satisfaction to either occupant or stray visitor is one of the axioms to be derived from a study of *Great Palaces*. But of course neither beauty nor comfort are the sole objects of this enquiry. It would be more honest to admit that we are looking for the quirks and foibles of the solar race. Take, for instance, the truckle beds of Franz-Josef at the Hofburg, at Schönbrunn, at the palace at Innsbruck, or in the Imperial villa at Bad Ischl. It is a part of history that he should 'retire' at 9 p.m. and 'rise' (like the Manchu Emperors) at 4 a.m., and while we do not envy him his ablutions in cold water and other hardships, to find him established on any one of thirty floors in a Hilton Hotel almost anywhere in the world would destroy the picture of the Hapsburg that we have in our minds.

Not that beauty, comfort or homeliness are missing from the scene, though the phrase *confort cossu*, familiar to readers of the *Guide Michelin*, is of rare application, meaning thereby unusual even in its own day. Looking down the whole list of Contents of *Great Palaces*, where else do these words apply but to Frederick the Great's Sans Souci? Versailles, the Alhambra, the Escorial might promise to be the most uncomfortable of the lot till we remember Caserta, the Quirinal or the (surely?) haunted rooms and passages of Holyroodhouse. And Queluz, beautiful but so furniture-less that we must imagine the court ladies, as Beckford describes them, sitting on the floor; or 'Mad King' Ludwig's Linderhof with its trip-up, toe-trap, professor-designed, gilt rococo which, as Baedeker says, 'will probably impress the modern visitor as artificial and exotic'. Looking merely at the façade of the Belvedere, in Vienna, where along that endless enfilade of windows with the domed towers standing like mitred grenadiers at the corners to dress the ranks, where, exactly, would you choose your bedroom to be? Or have you any desire to inhabit personally the royal palaces at Naples or Turin? It would be a bold spirit who accepted, even were those former palaces to be converted into flats.

There can be little doubt that the most agreeable of the royal residences herein depicted is Hampton Court, and this in spite of the rages and treacheries of Henry VIII by whose giant bulk the earlier, Tudor part of the building still seems inhabited, of the unprepossessing character and person of William III, builder of the Wren portions, and of the disagreeable dullness of four generations of the Hanoverian kings who inhabited the palace.

In what contrast the endless cardhouse of Versailles, ready, like a cardhouse, to fall in from both ends! But a magical transformation has taken place in the last few years and is still continuing, to culminate before long in the complete restoration of the bedroom of *Le Roi Soleil* with its gold hangings. Versailles, this dead capital of the civilised world, as it was indeed from 1660 until 1790, has come back to life.

If introduced, with some appreciation of works of art but no knowledge whatever of history, into the palace of Sans Souci at Potsdam, who would one surmise its builder and occupant to have been? Not, of a certainty, Frederick the Great, the military genius of his century, until, maybe, a door opened in the three-, or even four-toned gold snuff-box *boiseries*, and there entered, no maid of any kind, but an orderly, for the presence of females, we may feel sure, was dispensed with as far as possible in this society of young or ageing androgynes. There is the sense of such a regime in this exaggerated setting which goes beyond the normal. That this control-tower of a purposeful and ferocious militarism should house the delicate paintings by Watteau, and have been host to Voltaire, only makes stranger the mystery of Potsdam.

Italy, a land of town *palazzi*, is not at its best with royal palaces. Once the Medici were gone from Florence, the Hapsburg Archdukes of Tuscany made all they touched at the Pitti Palace into a poor imitation of the Hofburg at Vienna. It would take a dull pen to describe suitably the Palazzo Reale (of the Austrian Archdukes) at Milan, or the royal palace at Monza, both of them creations of Piermarini, a pupil of Vanvitelli. How different is, or was, the royal palace at Turin and its chain of apartments with ceiling-paintings by local artists, in further proof that this city and countryside with buildings by Juvara, by Guarini, by Vittone, is a land to itself and never quite either Italy, or France, or Spain!

Ludwig II's palace of Linderhof in Bavaria

Malmaison, the palace of Napoleon and Joséphine

The Royal Palace, Turin, in 1820

The Belvedere, Vienna, in the nineteenth century

A corner of the Quirinal, Rome

The Cour Royal at Versailles

The palace of the Escorial, Spain

But this land of princes rather than of kings contradicts itself in superb manner in the palace of Caserta. The monotonous splendour of the façade and of the garden beyond, which resembles the runway of an aerodrome handed back and planted by the municipal authorities with grass, has in supplement at the point of intersection of its four courts the marble vestibule that is like a stage-set by some designer of the Bibiena school made permanent in marble. Nothing better architecturally is dealt with in this present book. How many of the fine marbles of the classical world appear for another time upon this stair and landing, and has not the Palatine Theatre its twelve columns of *giallo antico* from the Serapeum at Pozzuoli? But this palace and garden, the last work of slaves, as it has been called – they were largely Barbary and Turkish slaves from off the galleys – diminishes in scale when we remember that the railway tunnels between San Remo and Pisa along the Mediterranean shore and between Bologna and Florence through the Apennines were the work of convict labour.

From Caserta to the Escorial is not so great a transition as might be imagined. Both the Escorial and Versailles were in the blood of its builder, Charles III, later King of Spain, who built, it could be said, an Escorial of his own within view of Vesuvius and cooled, as it were, by the waters and aqueduct of Marly. But we are in Iberia now, and where in the world is there anything more beautiful for the first and last half-hour than the Alhambra at Granada! Yet the marvellous intricacy of its bees' work in stucco, its stalactite and filigree pall and begin to bore, and in the end the beauty of the Alhambra is its red walls seen from below, and that bare hall with no decoration at all giving over the valley to the Albaicín.

More than just a touch of the Andalusian Moor persists in the palace of Sintra, in Portugal, where an Oriental flavour is given in the first instant by the two large conical chimneys of the medieval kitchen, reminiscent of the kitchen chimneys of the Janissaries at Istanbul. It is one of the amenities of the country round Lisbon that there is so wide a choice of climate in a small

The Royal Apartments at Windsor Castle

area, going from the mists and camellias of Sintra to the rough seas of Guincho, and from the massed bands of red geraniums at Estoril only a mile or two away to the narcissi'd hills of the peninsula across the Tagus. It is this entire unpredictability of expectation that gives charm to the pink palace of Queluz, and in stronger degree to the gardens than the palace, those gardens where Beckford heard, or says he heard, writing fifty years after that summer evening, a band of 'oboe and flute-players posted at a distance in a thicket of orange and bay-trees playing the soft *modinhas*' (popular songs) 'of Brazil'. Of all this book of palaces I would say that Queluz and Hampton Court and Sans Souci are the three that are on no account to be missed.

But our theme now turns northwards, and after Schönbrunn, where the clipped hedges and the golden coaches and the zoo are more worthwhile seeing than the interior of the palace, and after the Belvedere which once again is considerably more interesting outside than in – the caryatid staircase-hall excepted – we are making for the Baltic. Here, in Scandinavia, a first halt is at the Amalienborg, the diamond-shaped 'place' with palaces on its four main sides, a 'square' with only the Place Stanislas at Nancy for rival, and made more interesting in the knowledge that the one of these four palaces used by the Danish Royal Family as their residence has fine 'French' rooms and furniture.

The vast and barbaric enormity of the Russian royal palaces now obtrudes, but lightened when we know that the more than furlong-length façade of Tsarskoe Selo had every capital, vase and statue covered in gold-leaf in the time of Catherine, and that the long garden front was stained green, white and yellow. Inside are rooms encrusted with lapis-lazuli or with amber, and the famous bed-chamber of Catherine with its columns of purple glass, a *jeu d'esprit* on the part of Cameron, her Scots architect, to prove that costliness of material is not a necessity in architectural decoration. Lesser buildings at this old summer palace of the Tsars are no less interesting; as a Victorian writer put it, 'The odd caprices exhibited in the decoration of the grounds are really extraordinary, and so numerous that it would be difficult to enumerate them all', typical of which is a gateway to the palace flanked by triple rusticated columns topped by broken pediments, with chequered sentry-boxes much in evidence, and almost touching those, seated figures of Chinamen as from a fairground or off a tea-chest. After this, and more of the same kind, the story seems sane and probable that there should have been a sentry posted at one of the Russian palaces in the time of Catherine the Great to mount guard over a rose-tree, who was relieved, night and day, for more than a hundred years after the Empress was dead and the garden had been swept away.

SACHEVERELL SITWELL

The palace of Queluz, Portugal

A corner of Tsarskoe Selo, near Leningrad

Hampton Court

A fine combination of the Tudor and English baroque styles

The Clock Tower carries the astronomical clock which was made for King Henry VIII in 1540 by Nicholas Oursian

OPPOSITE: *The main entrance to Hampton Court, looking up to the Great Gate-house, which was originally a full storey higher*

HAMPTON COURT is a very big palace – so big that it is quite possible for two people to have clear and precise images of it, for both images to be correct and yet for each to be totally different. It is possible to remember Hampton Court as a Tudor palace and to forget that, as such, it has lost all its state apartments. It is possible to remember Hampton Court as a great work of Sir Christopher Wren and to forget that as such it is only a fragment of his whole design. Hampton Court shows us two architectural worlds, standing back to back, each robbing the other, but each so imposing as to carry absolute conviction.

The palace can be approached either from the Henry VIII end or from the William and Mary end. The Henry VIII end is near the river; seen across the water the palace provides the noblest panorama of Tudor architecture to be found anywhere, although the mind's eye must supply many more lead-tipped turrets and golden vanes than are there now. The gate-house is a modern reconstruction, but the court to which it leads is the Base Court built by Cardinal Wolsey soon after he obtained the site of the palace in 1514. The second gate-house is also Wolsey's – his arms stand over the arch – and it is from this court (the Clock Court) that some rooms which must have formed part of the Cardinal's private apartments are reached.

There is a room here known as Wolsey's Closet which is a peculiarly intimate and impressive relic of the man. The windows and doors are plain Tudor masonry. The panelling is the eternally repetitive linenfold. But above the panelling is a frieze of Renaissance paintings, while the ceiling is a fine elaboration

in gilded plaster of a pattern which has been traced back to Peruzzi's studio in Rome. Here is the essence of Wolsey – the plain English churchman who, nevertheless, made his sovereign the arbiter of Europe and who built and furnished Hampton Court to show foreign embassies that Henry VIII's chief minister knew how to live as graciously as any Cardinal in Rome.

Only fifteen years of Hampton Court belong to Wolsey. In 1529 he was passing over the whole establishment to the King when his disgrace was engineered, and in 1530 he died. Henry VIII proceeded with the building but increased its size and magnificence, building that range of state apartments which is now lost, together with his Conduit Court and his Queen's Gallery – the latter probably the model for hundreds of similar galleries – the 'long galleries' in which Elizabethans and Jacobeans took so much pleasure. Henry's Great Hall, however, survives. It fills the whole of the west side of Wolsey's Clock Court and fills it with great splendour because of its height and because the traceried windows, placed high in such high walls, leave an ample cliff of brick – diapered brick – below them. Internally, too, the hall is royally designed, with a roof of arched hammerbeam trusses, each twice arched to its neighbours, so that the whole roof is like a suspended miniature cathedral. It is beautifully enriched with renaissance ornament.

The Chapel is Wolsey's, but completed by Henry VIII with a timber and plaster ceiling in the form of a gothic pendant vault, with renaissance boys trumpeting from each pendant. The pendant theme occurs again, though less pretentiously, in the ceiling of the Watching Chamber. In the south wing of Clock Court are rooms full of Tudor panelling and with Tudor 'baton' ceilings in patterns of great elegance. In the north wing are the kitchens,

A drawing of Hampton Court in about 1557 by Wyngaerde, showing the original entrance tower and the Great Hall

Hampton Court in the seventeenth century before Wren's additions, which involved the demolition of many of the Tudor buildings seen in this view from the park side

An engraving of the palace showing the Tudor portion (the Base Court and the Clock Court) in the foreground and Wren's Fountain Court beyond. The River Thames borders the palace and its extensive park and gardens

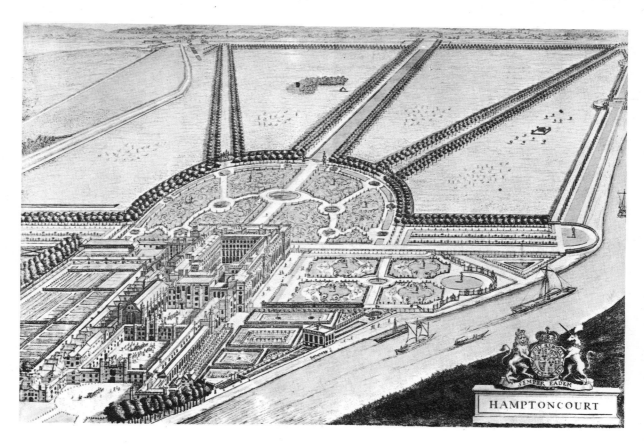

The palace in the early eighteenth century seen from the opposite direction to that illustrated above. The Great Fountain is in the foreground, and beyond it the east front of Wren's palace designed in the classical renaissance style

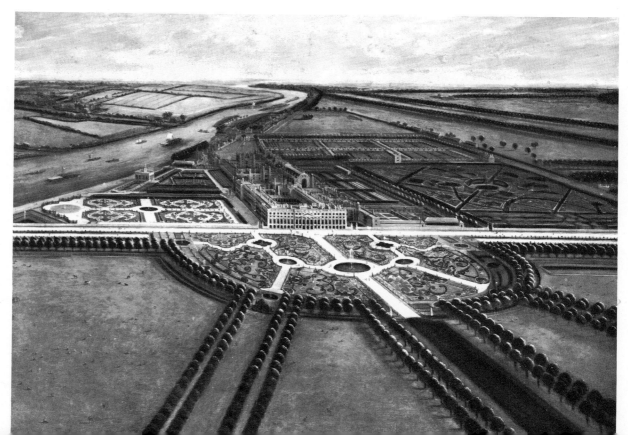

The two periods are evident from this air view. Left, Wolsey's palace (c. 1520) and, right, Wren's palace built in the late seventeenth century

OPPOSITE: *The Great Gate-house, with the arms of Henry VIII below the oriel window. The moat was filled in by order of Charles II and only re-excavated some fifty years ago*

spacious brick halls beautifully lit from windows too high to be looked out of. The Tudor palace spreads far, into courts and corridors not shown to sightseers, and into places where modest residences are occupied by persons of greater distinction than of wealth, who have the grace and favour of the Crown.

If the unspoiled Tudor character of much of Hampton Court is one of its greatest gifts to us, we owe it to the decision of William III to halt the rebuilding of the palace after the death of his Queen, Mary II, in 1694. In celebration of the Glorious Revolution which had brought them to the throne, William and Mary had been rebuilding rapidly since 1689 from the plans of their Surveyor of Works, Sir Christopher Wren, and these plans extended to a reconstruction of the entire palace, preserving only the Great Hall. Sir Christopher would have given us a palace with two great courts on two different axis, at right angles to each other; and the architecture of that palace would have been varied and delightful, with a domed silhouette and many subtle recollections of Mansart and Le Vau. The designs, in Wren's own hand, exist and one wonders why they were not carried out. A possible answer is that they did not quite sufficiently resemble Versailles. Versailles, as Le Vau left it in 1669, was impressive enough, but Jules Hardouin Mansart's extensions had been begun in 1674, and when William and Mary ascended the English throne in 1688 it was perhaps virtually

An anonymous painting of Henry VIII's meeting with François I at the 'Field of the Cloth of Gold' in 1520, which hangs in the King's Gallery

impossible for any sovereign to conjure up a palace in his imagination without seeing something akin to the stupendous monotony of the Versailles sky-line. Anyway, that is what Wren's mobile and ingenious silhouette had to give way to. Wren's park front at Hampton Court is nowhere near the extent of that of Versailles, but as far as it goes it is as flat-topped and as monotonous. True, the centre is laced with a Corinthian portico, but a portico helplessly embedded in the over-riding mass with its unstoppable rhythms. And when the park front turns the corner and becomes the Privy Garden front, nothing changes – everything repeats, almost to the point of tedium.

Almost, but not quite; Wren's Hampton Court fronts are not tedious because they are so exceedingly well modelled. Built of Portland stone and three kinds of brick, the mixing of these materials both as to colour and texture, the exact degree of relief in the architectural mouldings and the accent given by the naturalistic stone-carving unite in an amazingly fresh and successful result. Take a single bay of Versailles, consider it as a work of architecture and it will be found icily and uninterestingly efficient. Take a single bay of Hampton Court and there is a geniality and sensibility to which one always returns with pleasure and which does not diminish with repetition. It may be that the great sash-windows – among the first of their kind in England – have something to do with the peculiar geniality which so strongly pervades these great façades.

In the corner between the park and the Privy Garden fronts is the Fountain Court – a quadrangle in which the bay-unit of those fronts is repeated in a quicker rhythm and with the addition of pediments over the windows, so that the effect is rather startling, as of simultaneous exposure to a great many eyes, all

OPPOSITE: *The beautiful Fountain Court is part of the rebuilding of the palace by Sir Christopher Wren from 1689 onwards. The first-floor windows are those of the State Apartments which were designed for William III and Mary II and used by their successors until the accession of George III*

Two architectural worlds—
Henry VIII's Tudor
and Wren's baroque

RIGHT: *The geometrical pattern of ribs and pendants in the Watching Chamber*

ABOVE: *Inside Sir Christopher Wren's Ionic colonnade on the south side of the Clock Court*

ABOVE RIGHT: *One of the seventeenth-century classical portals on the first floor, with a balustrade of the same period*

RIGHT: *Part of the vast kitchen that provided Henry VIII's sumptuous banquets*

LEFT: *Part of Cardinal Wolsey's private suite of rooms, with its linenfold panelling, wall paintings and ornate ceiling*

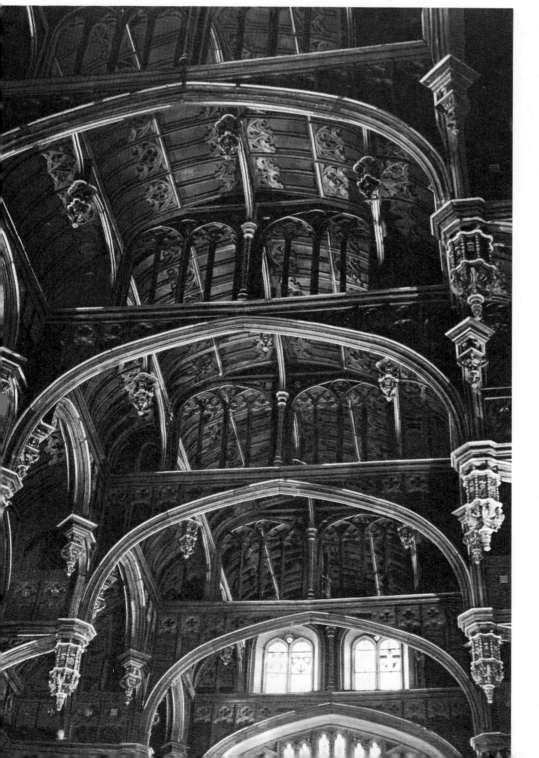

The Chapel Royal with its Gothic vault and renaissance pendants

LEFT: *The magnificently carved hammer-beam roof of the Great Hall, under which Henry VIII dined at a high table placed on a dais at the end*

A detail of Grinling Gibbons' carving

Wall-paintings by Antonio Verrio at the top of the King's Staircase

with raised eyebrows. An open cloister runs round the lower part of this court and brings us, at the north-west corner, to the Queen's staircase with its iron balustrade by Tijou and painted walls and ceiling. Up this stair we reach the Queen's Guard Chamber, the Presence Chamber and the long suite of apartments communicating with each other from end to end of the great park front and round to the Privy Garden front. These are the rooms lit by those splendid sash windows which account for so much of the character of the exterior. The interiors are remarkable for three things. First, for the painted ceilings, mostly the work of Verrio. Second, the rich and strikingly original fireplaces by Grinling Gibbons. Third, the works of art on the walls, which constitute a substantial and important section of the art collection of the British Crown.

But, paintings apart, the interiors of Wren's Hampton Court are not the things which leave the deepest impression. The gardens and fountains probably offer more to nearly everybody; and here Versailles is again reflected. To the north, towards Teddington, stretches the chestnut avenue of Bushy Park, planted exactly on the line which Wren chose for the greater (and unbuilt) part of his new palace. The Diana Fountain in Bushy Park is perhaps to Londoners in a very minor degree what the Bassin d'Apollon at Versailles is to Parisians. But the park-

A chandelier over the Queen's Staircase built for William and Mary

The mantelpiece by John Nost in the long gallery

lands at Hampton, though they have the discipline of Versailles, are demure and limited and there is time for the contemplation of detail – the baroque iron grilles of the Privy Garden, the carving on the piers of the Lion Gates, the decorative stone urns and lead vases. And, of course, the Maze.

Hampton Court is of two epochs – Tudor and Stuart; renaissance and baroque. Back to back they stand looking different ways both in time and space, blindly indifferent to each other and meeting only as a matter of convenience. In this juxtaposition are no accidental beauties, no unsought harmonies. And yet the whole vast building has something which, in the end, renders it a single artistic event. It is the notion of Triumph. Into his gate-towers Wolsey built terracotta heads of wreathed or helmeted Roman Emperors. A century later Charles I brought here Mantegna's *Triumph of Caesar*, now magnificently displayed in one of the orangeries. The theme of Triumph in full Roman accoutrements was taken up by William III's artists, and in the great pediment of the park front we see Hercules triumphing over Envy. Wherever we look, in Hampton Court, triumph is in the air. Of all the palaces of Britain it is the one which most consistently celebrates the success of British policy and the British Crown.

JOHN SUMMERSON

Windsor Castle

A fortress gradually converted into the residence of kings

WINDSOR CASTLE is a unique combination of a fortress, royal palace, a tomb of kings and queens and a glorious church in which the ideals of Christian chivalry are cherished and kept alive. This diversification of purpose is a fortuitous development, for it was as a stronghold to secure the western approaches to London that the Normans first chose this commanding site on a chalk outcrop above the Thames. The precise date of the construction of the first fortifications is not known, but Windsor Castle is mentioned in the Domesday Book of 1086 when it probably consisted of no more than the central keep, an artificial chalk mound fifty feet high surmounted by a wooden blockhouse. There were doubtless outlying palisades which would give adequate protection in an assault until the garrison could be mustered in the keep, where a deep well (still to be seen under the floor of a room in the Round Tower) would enable the defenders to withstand a siege.

It was Henry I who in 1110 first chose to convert this fortress into a royal residence, but of the buildings which he raised no identifiable trace remains. The earliest architectural features of Windsor Castle date from the reign of Henry II, who constructed a stone keep on the mound and fortified the exposed eastern flank with a row of towers which still exist, although greatly altered. It was as well he did, for shortly after his death in 1189 the castle suffered its first siege when the English barons attacked Prince John and his army of Welshmen. John escaped to France, but it was at Windsor that he resided as King during the humiliating week (June 15–23, 1215) in which he was forced to

The Garter and (beyond) the Curfew Towers at the north-west corner of the castle. The Curfew Tower dates from 1230, apart from its conical roof which was added in 1863

OPPOSITE: *From across the river at Eton College the Round Tower of the castle rises above the skyline*

WINDSOR CASTLE

A royal home for nearly nine centuries

OPPOSITE PAGE:

ABOVE LEFT *The south front from the Long Walk, a view opened up by George IV*
ABOVE RIGHT *The Round Tower was the original keep of the castle enlarged in the nineteenth century*
BELOW: *The East Terrace, overlooked by Queen Elizabeth's private apartments*

RIGHT: *St George's Chapel and the entrance to the Horseshoe Cloister*

St George's Chapel in the seventeenth century

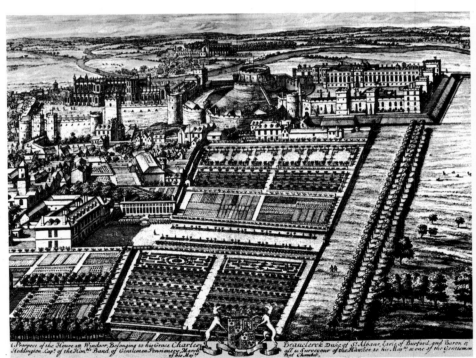

Windsor at the beginning of the eighteenth century. From Kips' Britannia Illustrata

LEFT: *An airview of Windsor Castle with the Round Tower in the centre*

Windsor in 1667

sign *Magna Carta* at Runnymede nearby. The following year the barons again besieged the castle but failed to take it in spite of the great siege engines which severely damaged the lower ward where there was still only a wooden palisade. Henry III immediately set about replacing the timber fortifications with a stout stone wall guarded by flanking towers. Much of his work is easily identifiable in the rough heath-stone courses of the wall beside the Curfew Tower.

The main difficulty in fortifying the castle was the complete absence of local stone, and the masonry of the Curfew Tower, built in 1230, is of massive chalk blocks. The exterior is now enclosed in a tidy granite case added in 1863 by the French architect Salvin, who built a sharply gabled roof in the style of his native castles. The interior of the tower is little altered and contains relics of the old gaol and a sally port or secret exit in case of siege. The upper part of the tower contains the castle bells placed there in 1478 and a clock of great ingenuity made by John Davis in 1689. Besides showing the time, this clock plays a psalm tune accompanied by merry peals every three hours.

Edward III was born at Windsor and it was he who endowed the castle with its great order of chivalry, the Order of the Garter. The founding of the order, according to the popular account, arose from a trivial incident about the year 1347; King Edward picked up from the ground a garter which had come adrift from the leg of the Queen or of 'some paramowre'. The King rebuked the ribald laughter of the courtiers by saying quietly: 'Sirs, the time shall shortlie come when yee shall attribute muche honour unto such a garter.' This royal reproof is perpetuated in the motto of the order: *Honi soit qui mal y pense.* The order seems originally to have been intended merely to form two teams for jousting, but the King's purpose quickly became more serious, for on August 6, 1348 he established the college of St George with a Custos and twenty-five canons and twenty-six 'Poor Knights', who were to attend mass daily as substitutes for the Companions of the Order of the Garter. This institution survives today, although on a reduced scale, with a dean, three canons and three minor canons; the Poor Knights, now thirteen in number and less bluntly called Military Knights, are retired officers of distinction.

Edward III had enlarged the chapel in the castle to accommodate his new order, but it was left to his namesake, Edward IV, to replace what was in 1472 a crumbling ruin by the present St George's Chapel with the magnificent tracery of its flat stone roof and the superb carved oak stalls for the Companions of the Order. The chapel was not completed until 1528 during the reign of Henry VIII, who was a popular figure at Windsor where he hunted in the forest and played tennis in a court (now disappeared) near the Round Tower. He was the first sovereign

A sixteenth-century battle-scene under the walls

The north-east angle in the eighteenth century

A nineteenth-century state reception at Windsor

OPPOSITE:

ABOVE *The Guard Chamber, hung with weapons and relics of various wars*
BELOW LEFT *The main terrace in the mid-eighteenth century, an engraving by John Brydell*
BELOW RIGHT *Holler's engraving of a state banquet in St George's Hall*

WINDSOR CASTLE

A bust of Queen Victoria in St George's Hall, below a portrait of William III (1688–1702) by Kneller

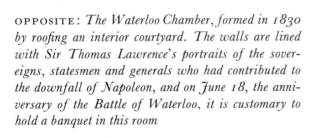

to be buried at Windsor, his body lying beneath the choir of St George's beside that of Jane Seymour. Charles I was also hastily buried in the same tomb in February 1649 when a few of his devoted followers were given permission to lay their sovereign to rest without ceremony of any sort.

Charles II, who had spent much of his youth in France, had plans to rival the splendour of Versailles at Windsor and built a complete new range of state apartments on the north terrace. The building was severely classical in style and entirely plain except for a huge Garter Star, but if the outside was austere, the interior was lavish in decoration with a mass of exuberant wood-carvings by Grinling Gibbons and Philipps, and twenty vast painted ceilings by Verrio of which only three now survive. In addition to this, Charles constructed a grand avenue stretching away to the south of the castle for three miles. A cluster of buildings prevented him from bringing the Long Walk up to the castle walls, but George IV, in 1824, had no scruples in demolishing all the houses, including one designed by his father. To compensate for this insult he commissioned specially a huge statue of George III dressed as a Roman Emperor, bestriding a gigantic

copper horse, which was erected at the far end of the Long Walk.

After a century of decay at Windsor, George IV transformed the castle to almost its modern appearance in a massive restoration and alteration undertaken by the architect Jeffry Wyatt, who improved his name to the more sonorous Wyatville in readiness for a knighthood. The work began in 1824 and continued for nearly sixteen years, during which time the whole upper and middle wards were made to look romantically Gothic by the addition of new and hideous windows, corbels and crenellations. Many of Wyatville's achievements can indeed be criticised as being both ugly and spurious, as for example the hollow wall, thirty feet high, added to the Round Tower, but it may be said in his defence that the symmetry of the castle as a whole is due entirely to his efforts, and as a result the distant view of Windsor Castle is magical.

Among the numerous interior changes was the building of the Waterloo Chamber in which portraits by Sir Thomas Lawrence commemorate monarchs, warriors and statesmen who contributed to the downfall of Napoleon. The idea originated with George IV who, as Prince Regent at the time of Waterloo, felt that he had played his part in ridding Europe of a tyrant. The result of this whim is a fine collection of portraits in a large room overpoweringly decorated, but containing such curiosities as a dining table capable of seating 150 persons and a seamless carpet, eighty feet by forty feet, woven in the prisons of Agra.

Another interior creation by Wyatville is the Grand Corridor, 550 feet in length, extending almost the whole way round the state and private apartments. It is not perhaps a handsome addition, but it was unquestionably necessary as a means of communication without having to cross the open courtyard which poor George III was obliged to do. The Grand Corridor became notorious during Queen Victoria's reign, for in this ill-heated tunnel ministers were forced to wait for an audience; here, too, guests stood after less formal dinners awaiting a summons to speak to the Queen, whose excellent circulation appeared proof against draughts.

The Prince Consort induced his wife to take up more or less permanent residence at Windsor, and during her reign the castle became virtually the centre of the Empire. From the uttermost parts of the earth, people of all races came to pay her homage: Indian princes who laid their swords at her feet, Singhalese whom the Queen thought exceedingly black, natives of British Guinea clad only in loincloths. All the crowned heads of Europe also came to Windsor and dared not misbehave in the presence of this dumpy widow who should have been comic or pathetic, but who exuded dignity and authority.

Since Queen Victoria's death in 1901 it has been customary for the court to reside at Windsor only at Easter and during the

An angle of the Grand Staircase, on which stands a marble statue by Sir Francis Chantry (1781–1842) of George IV, to whose taste and bold restorations in the 1820's so much of the present appearance of the State Apartments is due. Below it stands the sturdy suit of English armour made at Greenwich for King Henry VIII in about 1540

week of Ascot races. It is during these short periods that the state apartments cease to be a museum through which hordes of sight-seers tramp daily and revert to the purpose for which they were created by Charles II and George IV. In the Second World War Windsor Castle resumed its role of a fortress where the Royal Family lived secure from enemy bombs and yet close to London to discharge their manifold wartime duties. Since the accession of Queen Elizabeth II, the castle has been used frequently at week-ends by the Royal Family, who enjoy riding in the Great Park, and it is fitting that they should continue to reside in the castle from which, since 1917, their name derives and which has been the home of the monarchy for close on nine centuries.

B. J. W. HILL

Looking through the door of the Grand Reception Room to the Garter Throne Room, in which the cere-monies of the Order of the Garter are conducted

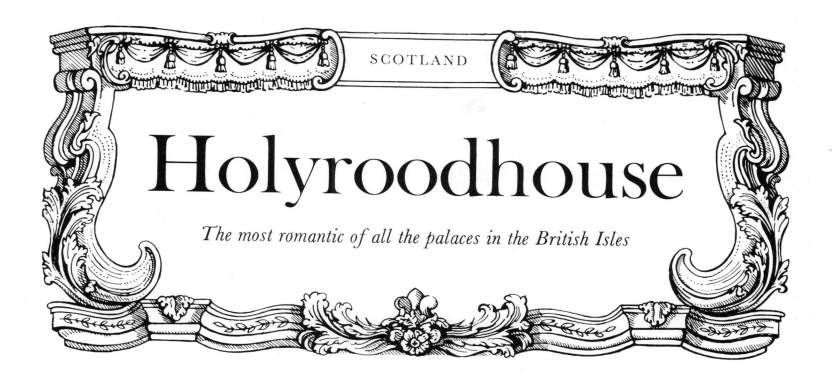

Holyroodhouse

The most romantic of all the palaces in the British Isles

IF YOU WALK DOWN BETWEEN the soaring grey skyscrapers of old Canongate from west to east, you come in the end to the Palace of Holyroodhouse, which lies half in Edinburgh and half in the bald grey wilderness that rises to Arthur's Seat. It is architecturally perhaps not very exciting to most people, though it is an interesting and an elegant building, but its associations with Mary, Queen of Scots, with the Young Pretender, and with Charles X in his penniless exile, make it by far the most romantic of the British royal palaces. There are several legends about its founding, and historically the most probable is the following: St Margaret, the second Queen of Malcolm Canmore and the sister of Edgar Atheling, brought with her to Scotland in 1068, a gold casket in the shape of a cross, covered by an ebony carving of the Saviour and containing a sizable piece of the True Cross. This casket, known as the Black Rood of Scotland, came eventually to her son David I, and, as one of his people's most precious emblems, was given for safe-keeping to the monks of a new abbey that he had founded at Edinburgh in 1128. The abbey became known as Holyrood, though the casket was taken to Durham by the English two centuries later, and was lost at the Reformation. Holyrood had a guest-house often used by the kings of Scotland. James II was born, crowned, married and buried there, and James III married Margaret of Denmark in the abbey. Their son, James IV, handsome, wilful, brave, and intellectually far the most gifted Scottish king, decided to build a palace at Holyrood. It was begun in 1501, and in 1504 James brought to his new home, his queen, Margaret Tudor, daughter

The ruins of the Augustinian abbey, founded by King David I in 1128, with the seventeenth-century building alongside it

OPPOSITE: *The entrance gates facing the two turrets which formed part of the original palace. On the left are part of the ruins of the Abbey Church which became the Chapel Royal*

35

of Henry VII. His palace was the present north-west tower. Ten years later he lay dead at Flodden 'in the dark impenetrable wood of Scottish spears'. Under James V, with his two French queens, Madeleine, daughter of François I, and Margaret of Guise, a Renaissance façade, looking to the west and centring on a great gateway, was added. In 1542 the King died, leaving a week-old daughter, Mary, Queen of Scots.

Henry VIII planned that she should marry his son Edward, and in July 1543 a marriage treaty was signed at Greenwich. Six months later the Francophile Scottish parliament annulled the treaty and an infuriated Henry sent the future Lord Protector Somerset on the expedition called the 'Rough Wooing', to sack Edinburgh 'and so deface it as to leave a memory for ever of the vengeance of God upon their falsehood and disloyalty'. He fired the abbey and James' new palace. The abbey roof resisted the flames, but three years later Somerset returned, stripped the lead from the roof and left it to decay. The nave was reroofed and used till James II's time as the parish church of the Canongate. Mary of Guise, who had become Regent during her daughter's minority, had the palace restored.

Her daughter, Mary, who had been sent to France, educated there, married to the Dauphin, and been Queen of France for a year, returned as a widow of eighteen to live as Queen of Scots at Holyroodhouse. She must have been very happy to be back in Scotland, wandering with her four Maries along the pleached alleys and flagged paths of the Holyrood gardens, but it was a short idyll which ended abruptly with her marriage to her cousin Lord Darnley and the murder of her secretary, David Rizzio, who clung pleading to her skirts till her husband's accomplices cut him down. There followed the terrible drama of the explosion at Kirk O' Field, where Darnley's body was found unscarred beneath a tree in the garden, and finally her marriage in the abbey to Lord Bothwell who was openly rumoured to be the murderer of her husband. Meanwhile, the future James I of England had been born in Edinburgh Castle. Three weeks after her marriage to Bothwell, his mother left Holyrood for ever for the series of 'strange tragedies' predicted by John Knox which led to her defeat at Carberry Hill, her abdication, her escape from Loch Leven helped by her young adorer William Douglas, her flight to England, and her imprisonment and execution at Fotheringay. Young James VI lived on at Holyrood till he became the rheumy doting King James I of England in 1603. He came once only to Scotland after his succession, but his son, Charles, came in 1633 to be crowned in the abbey and the master mason, John Mylne, made, to celebrate the occasion, the stone sundial now in the garden, carved with the ciphers of the young king and Henrietta Maria. In 1650, while Cromwell's soldiers were quartered there after the battle of Dunbar, fire swept the palace,

A drawing of Edinburgh with 'the Kyng of Skotts Palas' in 15

An engraving by de Wet before the reconstruction of the palace

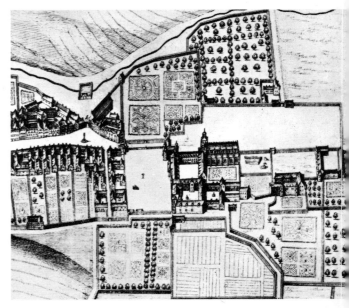

The Holyroodhouse section of a bird's-eye view of Edinburgh

almost destroying it, and it took the next nine years to rebuild it.

At the restoration, Charles II ordered a complete reconstruction of his Scottish palace. Cromwell's west façade was replaced by a two-storey building centring on a great Doric gateway and ending in a tower to balance James IV's. The gateway, which bears the arms of the kings of Scots and the thistle motto *Nemo me impune lacessit*, and rises to a stone lantern covered by a pierced crown, leads to an arcaded stone quadrangle of four storeys, ninety-four feet square. The first floor consists of an enfilade of state rooms and the second floor is given over to a suite of rooms, where the Royal Family live when they are in Edinburgh. Walking into this tall elegant courtyard, one imagines oneself in some small Marot palace in Amsterdam or in the *hôtel particulier* of some Louis XIV soldier of fortune behind the Place des Vosges, never for a moment in a Scottish royal palace. Inside, the high tapestried walls, Delft-tiled fireplaces, and beautiful pompous ceilings by the Fleming, de Wet, add to the feeling of some small town palace in the Netherlands.

As we see it today the palace dates almost entirely from this rebuilding. Its three many-windowed storeys divided by groups of flattened pilasters, Doric and Ionic for the first two storeys, and finally Corinthian, and topped by a shallow mansard with

IOANNES CNOXVS.

John Knox, the only authentic portrait existing

LEFT: *The west front, by Charles II's architect, Sir William Bruce*

Mary, Queen of Scots. A copy of the portrait by Clouet in the Royal Collection

LEFT: *A painting by Roderick Chalmers showing the different types of craftsmen engaged upon the repairs*

The north-west tower was built in about 1500 by James IV. The drainpipe bears evidence of George IV's restorations three hundred years later

A mingling of the thirteenth century with the seventeenth. Flying buttresses cross Charles II's façade

OPPOSITE: *The interior courtyard built by Charles II during his reconstruction of the palace*

batteries of tall chimneys, would have passed unnoticed on the Continent, but to Scottish eyes must have seemed a great innovation. Levau had done similar things a decade earlier at the Louvre, and Wren and Talman were to follow suit fifteen years later, but here, for the first time, one can see a significant architectural result of the long Franco-Scottish alliance.

The King's architect was Sir William Bruce of Balkaskie, a young Scottish adventurer, whose pains as go-between of General Monke to the young Charles in exile, had been rewarded with the lucrative Clerkship of the Bills. Robert Mylne, who had followed his father, John, designer of the dead King's coronation sundial, prepared a scheme with Sir William, which the Duke of Lauderdale took to the King, and in 1671 Bruce was made King's Surveyor and Master of Works.

To aid him Bruce had two very good plasterers, John Houlbert and George Demsterfield, the Flemish painter de Wet and a brilliant woodcarver John van Santvoort. Shipments of Delft tiles, lead, carved wainscoating, and linseed oil came from Rotterdam, and nine marble fireplaces from London. De Wet, beside several ceilings and overmantels, painted a series of portraits of the kings of Scotland to decorate the long gallery. Poor Bruce was by no means given *carte blanche*, and the Lords Commissioners to the Treasury were stern critics of his extravagance! 'His Majesty', they wrote, 'thinks the way proposed for the inner court would be very noble, but will not go to that charge, and therefore his pleasure is that it be plain ashlar, as the front is, with table divisions for storeys.' However, in 1679 the palace was finished and James, Duke of York, lived there as Lord High Commissioner.

In 1687, two years after he succeeded as King, he determined that Scotland should be Roman Catholic, and enforced an enactment of 1672 that the abbey church should become His Majesty's chapel royal, and headquarters of the newly revived Knights of the Thistle, and that the Canongate parishioners should find themselves a new church. The abbey was fitted out as a Catholic chapel, and part of the palace was given over to a seminary for Scottish priests. In the revolution that followed the landing of William of Orange, both were sacked, and drunken presbyterians burst open the tombs of the kings of Scotland, and made bonfires of missals and vestments. When the Act of Union was passed in 1707, Holyrood sank into oblivion, to wake once a year for the annual visit of the Lord High Commissioner. It emerged for a few weeks of transient glory, when the Young Pretender came in 1745, and the Long Gallery was given over to a grand ball, but within months 'Butcher' Cumberland was there in his stead, and the Stuart star had set for good. After the French Revolution another exile came to Holyrood. A set of rooms in the delapidated palace (the abbey had been in total

ABOVE: *The plasterwork in the part of the palace built during the seventeenth century was executed by John Houlbert and George Demsterfield, and is of outstanding quality*

OPPOSITE: *The Music Room, one of the State Apartments designed as a royal suite for Charles II, contains an elegant harpsichord of 1636*

ruin since the roof collapsed in 1768) was given to the Comte d'Artois. The Abbé Egeworth, who had consoled Louis XVI at the scaffold, visited his brother and tells how he left the palace only on Sunday for fear of being arrested for debt, and sat in the morning room gazing at a little gouache painted by his favourite sister, Madame Elizabeth, of a harbour scene. This picture now belongs to the Duke of Buccleuch.

George IV paid his famous visit to his northern capital in 1822. He was the first British king to set foot on Scottish soil for over a hundred years, and in honour of his visit the forecourt was paved with Kensington gravel, and a room provided with a Grecian couch, hung with white satin. Prinny was bewitched enough to get a government grant of £24,000 to set Holyrood to rights. The Comte d'Artois returned in 1830 as Charles X, once again seeking refuge from his creditors (and this time also his subjects), and brought with him the Duchesse de Berri and the young Comte de Chambord. With them also came their chef Monsieur Santad, whose son Alphonse, would chant through the wynds of the Canongate royalist tags like *Napoléon et Louis-Philippe sont des grands cochons.*

Albert and Victoria came in 1852 and they and their successors each added something to the beauty of the palace. In the evening drawing-room are Brussels tapestries of the continents given by Queen Victoria from Buckingham Palace, and in her old drawing-room are the Paris tapestries of the exploits of Diana woven after Toussaint Dubreuil. Victoria also gave the Darnley memorial picture, which had come from the Lennoxes, by way of Lord Pomfret to George II. It shows his family praying for vengeance on his murderers. His catafalque is in the background and there is an inset painting of the rout of Mary's army at Carberry Hill. It now hangs in the west drawing-room, panelled by George V in 1911 out of wood from an oak tree, felled at Yester in Midlothian, which provided 591 cubic feet of usable timber – a rather hideous piece of virtuosity.

Although there is a general impression inside of tall tapestried saloons and writhing plaster-work, there is much that disappoints. The furniture is for the most part ordinary and unbeautiful. It is specially sad that there is so little left to help one to imagine the palace of Mary and her four Maries. True, there is the ceiling in the old tower with the ciphers and emblems of the Dauphin, François I and Mary of Guise, but the Queen's bed is seventeenth-century and so is most of the furniture in her rooms. Despite these shortcomings, it is in any mood a lovely and romantic place, where one can always feel the troubled Stuart past and the proud independence of the Scots.

CHRISTOPHER GIBBS

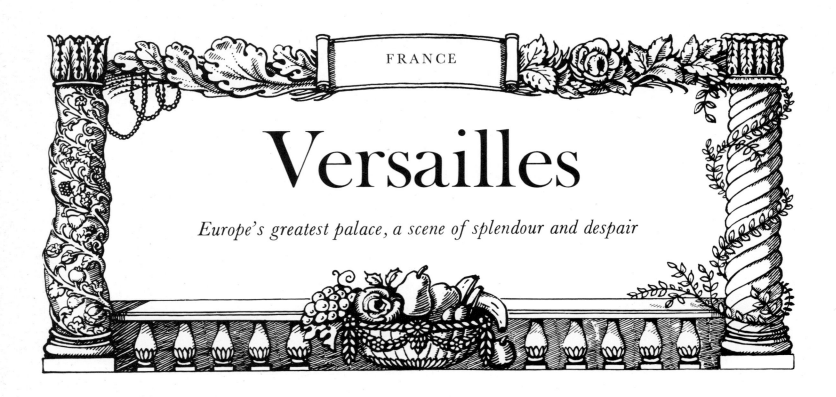

Versailles

Europe's greatest palace, a scene of splendour and despair

An equestrian statue of the Duc d'Orléans (1810–42) by M. Marochetti. It was originally erected in 1844 in the courtyard of the Louvre and now stands outside the Orangerie at Versailles

OPPOSITE: *The Cour Royale, looking towards the chapel and the Gabriel wing. The chapel, built in white stone, was begun by Mansart in 1699, but was not completed until 1710, two years after his death*

HISTORY SEEMS TO SELECT certain places, hitherto unknown, as appropriate settings for memorable events and scenes of splendour and shame. Looking back, the historian can see some connection between the name of such a place, its geographical position and the part it played in history. The fact that Versailles is built on a hill, and that the slopes that fall away on one side are covered in gardens while those that drop down on the other form one of the most impressive semi-circular approaches known to any royal residence, has frequently led men to think that the name 'Versailles' is derived from the word *versant*, a slope. Though this idea may well be the result of an etymological fad prevalent at the time, it is perfectly true that Versailles was the summit of that slope down which the French monarchy tumbled to its ruin. Here man had tried to master nature; in its own indirect way nature took its revenge upon man – indeed, could not this death-blow to the French monarchy be nature's retaliation upon the men who had tried to subdue her and to turn what was once a swampy hunting ground covered with bushes into some of the most magnificent gardens that the world has ever seen? Neither Saint-Simon nor Colbert showed any sign of enthusiasm for Versailles, and Saint-Simon, were he still with us, could congratulate himself on his foresight in describing Versailles as 'the gloomiest and most barren of places; it has no view, no woods, no water, no soil; for it is nothing but marshes and shifting sands'.

The Duke's acid comments can be countered by the claim that Versailles represents a great victory of man over nature.

VERSAILLES

The very conception of erecting such a palace with such superb grounds in so desolate a spot could only have occurred to a man who thought of himself as invested with a God-given right to do so and to raise up out of nothing a residence that still astonishes us today. The whole history of Versailles is a juxtaposition of opposites. Deeds of the blackest hue coincide with the splendour and glitter of *le Roi Soleil*. There is, for instance, *l'Affaire des Poisons* (the Poisons Case) which ended in the Marquise de Brinvilliers' condemnation to torture and death for having slowly poisoned her father, her two brothers and some accomplices in order to get money for the man she loved. That was in 1670. In 1784 occurred *l'Affaire du Collier* (the Affair of the Queen's Necklace), and these two events in two successive centuries changed the court for a while from a seat of pleasure into a hot-bed of Machiavellian plotting and intrigue. As the power of Louis XIV grew, so did the brilliance of his court, but in his old age it became so gloomy and forbidding, that no sooner had he died than the court fled to Paris.

Wonderful celebrations were held in Versailles to mark the birth of princes of the blood yet subsequent events contrasted darkly with this early promise. Of the four monarchs who were born there – Louis XV, Louis XVI, Louis XVIII and Charles X – the second died in tragic circumstances, the third was an exile before coming to the throne and the last was an exile after losing the throne. Two Dauphins were born there as well, and the crown was snatched from both, by the untimely death of the first and by the particularly horrible death of the second.

Versailles was the scene of jubilation over glorious victories – those won by Condé over the Imperial troops in 1674 – but it was the scene of bitter shame too, as in 1871 when the proclamation of the German Empire marked an ignominious French defeat. In 1919 a new page was turned and the stigma of 1871 was wiped out by the signature of the Treaty of Versailles.

Still further contrasts are to be found here. From the glittering round of entertainment given by Louis XIV, (*Les Plaisirs de l'Ile enchantée*, 1664) the mind cannot but turn to the *Banquet des Gardes* which sparked off the explosion of the French Revolution on October 4, 1789. Again, the mental image of the crowds who flocked to see the *Roi Soleil* must be followed by that of the mob that came to drag Louis XVI back to Paris.

This palace, that for sheer size stands alone in the western world, is full of antitheses. Though its last owner dedicated it TO ALL THE GLORIES OF FRANCE yet the fate of the men who lived there seems to turn it into an illustration of the harsh statement: SIC TRANSIT GLORIA MUNDI. All the past is woven of light and shade, of splendour and despair, and it is the intermingling of these through the years that gives Versailles its aura of majesty and its unique position in French history.

The south end of the central block of the palace (1678–81), built by Mansart soon after he came to work for Louis XIV at Versailles

RIGHT: *The entrance gate into the Cour Royale, with the statue of Louis XIV by Petiot and Cartellier in the centre*

Detail of the north façade of the Cour de Marbre. The structure is that of Louis XIII's original hunting-lodge

RIGHT: *The Cour de Marbre, which was embellished with but gilded balconies and pediments in the late seventeenth century*

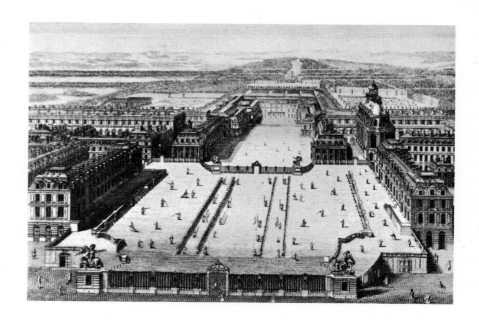

A seventeenth-century engraving of a parade held in the main entrance to the château after the huge building had been completed

OPPOSITE: *The central block of the palace seen across the Parterre du Midi. This large construction was the work of Louis Le Vau between 1668 and his death in 1670. The façade was criticised in the eighteenth century for its monotony and the use of the Ionic order for so large a building. But originally the two upper storeys were set back, leaving a huge terrace above the rez-de-chaussée*

The real story of Versailles opens with a windmill on a hill and a hunting party – of which the young king, Louis XIII, was a member – in the woods nearby. So marked an impression did this make on the young king that eighteen years later, in 1624, he bought the knoll and built a small hunting box there, which was the origin of the future palace. This was the scene of the *Journée des Dupes* (the Day of the Dupes) in 1630. On this occasion Louis XIII, in spite of the efforts of Marie de' Medici who wanted to dismiss Richelieu from his high office, asserted his authority and assured the Cardinal of his continued support and favour. In 1632 Louis XIII purchased the Manor of Versailles from its owners, the Gondis, to whom it had belonged since 1572. He took over the whole estate and committed to Philibert

Versailles seen from the Cour de Marbre by J-B Martin. The great stables, which were built by Mansart, 1679–80, lie on either side of the main avenue

André Le Nôtre, after a painting by Marat. Le Nôtre was employed by Louis XIV to transform the gardens at Versailles, and he succeeded in creating the greatest garden in the world by adapting his geometric designs to the lie of the land

BELOW: *Louis XIV receiving the Ambassadors of Siam in audience at Versailles in 1686*
BELOW RIGHT: *Louis XIV (seated) and his family, the Dauphin, the Duc de Bourgogne and the Duc de Bretagne (the elder son of the Duc de Bourgogne) with his governess. A conversation piece by Nicolas de Largillière (1656–1746)*

le Roy the task of improving the hunting-lodge which was to remain his favourite resort until his death in 1643.

From 1661 onwards, the young Louis XIV started adding to this favourite property of his father's. He increased the size of the estate, embellished the buildings, made Le Nôtre responsible for the planning and design of the park, ordered the Grand Canal to be cut and had the servants' quarters enlarged. In 1668 he commissioned the architect Le Vau to extend the country house, while keeping the original nucleus intact, and to turn it into a palace fit for such as he, a scion of the Medici. Le Vau's great innovation was to build the terraces. But the architect who gave Versailles its present appearance was Jules-Hardouin Mansart. Between 1678 and 1708 he completely transformed the palace, giving it its present façade on to the gardens, its Galerie des Glaces, its Grand Commun, its Chapel and its North and South Wings. Such extensions were necessary because at first only the king and his court lived at Versailles. Later the seat of government was transferred from St Germain to Versailles and government officials came to swell the crowd of courtiers already thronging the palace. Finally, many changes were effected inside the palace and the Orangery was constructed; its size filled the Siamese ambassadors with astonishment.

The Opera House was built under Louis XV by Jean-Ange Gabriel from 1757 to 1770. It was first used on the occasion of the wedding of the Dauphin (the future Louis XVI) and Marie-Antoinette. Gabriel also designed the wing in the courtyard that bears his name. It was to balance this that, after the recall of the Bourbon House, another wing was added on the left. Mansart had built the Grand Trianon in 1687; J. A. Gabriel erected the Petit Trianon between 1762 and 1770. The last small building to be erected, the Hameau, was finished only three years before the Revolution. Versailles is thought to have cost between seventy and one hundred million pounds.

When the visitor, arriving from Paris, reaches the huge star-shaped approach that extends in front of the palace, he cannot fail to be impressed by the splendour of the edifice before him,

One of the chandeliers in the Salon de la Guerre

An oval bas-relief by Coysevox of the victorious Louis XIV

OVERLEAF: *The Galerie des Glaces was constructed between 1678 and 1684 on Le Vau's exterior terrace. About 240 feet long, the Galerie is lit by seventeen great windows reflected in the mirrors opposite. The decorations were designed by Charles Le Brun. In its days of glory, the Galerie, illuminated by 3,000 candles, formed a brilliant setting for festivities and Court ceremonies. It was here that the Treaty of Versailles was signed in 1919*

The Galerie des Glaces was Mansart's finest achievement in the interior

by its symmetry and by its air of majesty. If he follows the irregular paving between the wings of the building and goes towards the Cour de Marbre, he will feel as if he were approaching a temple. This was the spot Louis XIV chose for his bedroom – as if he had wanted the splendour of the rising sun each morning to reflect his own brilliance. And yet it was on this very balcony that Marie-Antoinette stood and was cheered for the last time by the mob that had come to break into the palace, but whose fury was for a moment held spellbound by her charm.

'Leave the château by the hall leading into the Cour de Marbre and go out on to the terrace. Stop for a moment at the top of the steps and gaze at the way the flower beds are laid out, at the ornamental lakes and at the fountain . . .'. This is the advice given by Louis XIV in the heading of his book *Manière de montrer les Jardins de Versailles*. Seen from the terrace the park is perfectly laid out and the symmetry is complete: the flower beds are in harmonious balance with each other, groves and walks are skilfully mingled and ornamental lakes follow one another in perfect geometrical pattern. 'Gardens that have become

palaces,' wrote La Fontaine, realising that the gardens had been planned with such care that their design seemed to have influenced the very shape of the palace itself, since Le Vau and Mansart undoubtedly followed the pattern set by Le Nôtre. As if by magic Le Nôtre had turned mire into fountains, mud into thickets and marshy ground into pools of water before Vauban came to organise the magnificent water display. To the left stands the Orangery with its double flight of steps, known as the Cent Marches, to the right lies the Bassin de Neptune, in direct line with the Pièce d'Eau des Suisses. The long stretch of lawn, l'Allée du Tapis Vert, with quincunx arrangement of trees on either side, runs from the Bassin de Latone to the Bassin d'Apollon which leads on to the Grand Canal. This incredibly smooth sheet of water, nearly a mile long, used to be the scene of Louis XIV's boating parties. On these occasions, gorgeous displays would be given and the Grand Canal would be criss-crossed by fleets of Venetian gondolas, tiny frigates and brigantines.

There is much to see on the way back. The Bosquet de la Colonnade should not be missed, for it is the only one to retain its original aspect, while the Bosquet de la Reine and that of the Bains d'Apollon should certainly be seen, as should the Bassin de Neptune with its baroque sculpture. From there the Allée des Marmousets should be followed right up to the Parterre d'Eau. Viewed from this slight distance the immense façade of the château looks for a moment like one continuous line of incredible length, extending as it does for 634 yards.

Many a visitor, on entering the silent palace today, would echo the words of one of the great ladies of Louis XIV's time who, on coming to Versailles during the King's absence, replied to a questioner who asked if she did not consider Versailles the most enchanting of places, 'Yes, if the enchanter were here'. Yet in spite of the fact that those magnificent candelabra, masterpieces of the goldsmiths' work during the baroque period, are no longer there and although some of the most beautiful pieces of furniture have now gone, the spirit of Louis XIV still lingers everywhere. Magnificence, light and majesty are the hall-marks of the palace. The interior decoration endeavours to imitate the sun, and the ceilings are covered with gold after the fashion of the heavenly body the King chose as his symbol. 'In all things he loved brilliance, splendour, profusion. His taste for these he deemed it politic to adopt as a golden rule with which to imbue his court', said Saint-Simon. In addition, he was very conscious of his own high majesty, and this is glorified everywhere. Mignard's picture of Louis XIV on horseback is the first thing to strike the visitor on entering the Salon d'Hercule. The sole purpose of the state rooms seems to be to extol him – in the Salle de Diane there is his bust by Bernini, in the Salon de Mars Le Brun's tapestry exalts his military prowess, in the Salon de la

A trophy in the Salon de Diane

The Queen's Staircase, by which the revolutionaries entered in 178

The palace seen from the Tapis Vert

A gilded gate, surmounted by the Sun King's emblem

Guerre a bas-relief by Coysevox shows him trampling his enemies underfoot, and – everlasting theme, endlessly painted, carved or engraved – a monogram of his initial entwined with itself. The sole purpose of this suite of state rooms is to lead up to the long Galerie des Glaces. This splendid hall has seventeen large windows overlooking the park. The reflection of the view seen through them is immediately caught by seventeen tall mirrors on the wall opposite. But this, magnificent though it be, is not all. The ceiling, too, sparkles with the tale told in gold of all the glorious feats of the reign, feats which Le Brun has skilfully told under the guise of allegorical myths.

The King's Bedroom comes immediately between this enchanted haven of reflections and the Cour de Marbre, on the exact line that would join the Grand Canal and the Avenue de Paris. To have placed the room here seems like an echo of the King's words: 'Since we are God's divine agent it is fitting that we should share in His wisdom as well as in His authority'. The choice of such a spot for the strict ritual of the *lever* and *coucher* was a source of astonishment to Spanish visitors who had expected to find a chapel at this focal point.

To reach the chapel the visitor, after first glancing at the Queen's State Apartments to the south, must cross Louis XV's room and note in passing how attractive it is – a true reflection of an age when indulgence in pleasure was more sought after than winning glory in the field of honour. He will then come to the north wing which contains firstly the chapel and lastly the Opera House. Though one was built in the time of Louis XIV and the other during the reign of Louis XV the difference between them is not as great as the contrast between the two reigns. In fact it is difficult to decide which of the two – the chapel or the Opera House – is the better fitted as a stage for spectacular performances and theatrical ostentation. As for finding a suitable place for meditation, this or that box at the Opera would provide a more conducive setting than would the royal gallery where Louis XIV was wont to appear at Mass facing the tiers of seats erected for the choirs and orchestra.

The best conclusion would seem to be contained in these words of Bossuet's: 'Sire, some great and powerful force is at work on Your Majesty's behalf which will lift you far above any king who came before you'. It would seem that this exordium pronounced at the beginning of his reign was remembered by Louis XIV and inspired him to conceive the idea of erecting such a stately background for his achievements and so enduring a monument to his greatness. For a century this palace was to be the prototype of royal and princely residences before its layout was adopted by newly made capitals like Washington and St Petersburg.

JEAN-DOMINIQUE REY

Malmaison

The favourite country residence of Napoleon and Joséphine

Napoleon at Malmaison. A portrait by Gérard painted at the château in the year of his coronation

OPPOSITE: *Joséphine's circular bedroom in which she died, with its slim gilded pillars backed by fabric*

MALMAISON IS NOT A palace. Yet Napoleon lived there during the dawn and the decline of his tumultuous career; Joséphine loved it, improved it, and when destiny turned against her, retired there and finally died there. And so, by virtue of its owners, Malmaison deserves a place here.

It was a charming residence, built about 1620, just outside the village of Rueil, and it had been inhabited in turn by several families, the last of which was the Le Couteux de Moley. Abbé Delille described the stream which crossed the park in verse and regretted not having spoken more of this delightful spot in his poems on 'Gardens'. Madame Vigée-Lebrun, who dined there in 1789 with Abbé Sieyès and several other enthusiasts of the Revolution, told how: 'Mr de Moley inveighed against the nobles; everyone shouted, held forth . . . Abbé Sieyès said: In fact I believe we shall go too far.'

The Revolution ended, the Le Couteux lost their fortune. Their home was sacked and they were glad to sell it. It was all on her own that Joséphine chose it and bought it in 1799 while her husband was waging war in Egypt, and he settled the payment on his return. When he became First Consul he took up residence at the Tuileries 'sad in its magnificence', but often escaped to rejoin Joséphine who had established herself at Malmaison with her daughter, Hortense. He went there on the Decade, the tenth day of the Revolutionary week (equivalent to our week-end), and indeed whenever he could get away. The days he spent there were his holidays, said Bourrienne.

After all the atrocities of the Revolution, after the ostentatious

The garden façade of Malmaison. At the entrance between the obelisks Napoleon erected a tent-like structure to avoid too abrupt a transition from the drive to the entrance hall

and somewhat vulgar festivities of the Directory – Bonaparte being First Consul – it was, in fact, Malmaison that promoted a certain *douceur de vivre*. What fun it must have been for those hitherto unaccustomed to power and luxury to ride in smart carriages dressed in all their finery, to give lovely balls for beautiful women, to acquire – with all that that implied – elegance! Napoleon, still young and gay (he was only thirty), had not outgrown the mischievousness of his Corsican boyhood. They played Prisoners' Base, Blind Man's Buff and Backgammon and they also arranged amateur theatricals under the auspices of Talma. Whenever the weather permitted, they dined outside on the lawn.

Madame Bonaparte gardened. If history has judged her frivolous, extravagant, unfaithful, flirtatious, and all the rest, we must allow her two qualities; she loved to do good and she took up gardening seriously. To the latter role she applied herself with a consistency that she has so often been accused of lacking. Indeed it was thanks to her care that the gardens of Malmaison became famous. She built an enormous greenhouse up against an old pavilion, and there she accommodated some of the horticultural scientists and botanists with whom she surrounded herself, among them André du Pont, Cels, Guerrapain, Vilmorin,

OPPOSITE: *The reception room at Malmaison in which hang the two portraits of Napoleon and Joséphine reproduced in detail on pages 54 and 63*

57

the Chevalier Soulange-Bodin, and also an English colleague, Kennedy. There was also a drawing room in the greenhouse where she liked to sit and where Gérard painted her portrait. Here, and in the park, laid out in the English style, she collected the rarest trees and the most exotic flowers. These came to her from all over the world, many from the Antilles, her native islands. The corvettes *Géographe* and *Naturaliste* brought back shiploads of plants and seeds. The First Consul wrote to his wife in 1801 (year IX): 'I have received some plants for you from London and I have sent them to your gardener.' This was a courteous gesture from the Prince Regent. Thus rhododendrons, myrtle, mimosa, cacti, phlox, catalpa, hibiscus enriched her collection. She had a predilection for the roses Redouté came to paint on the spot and she had some rose trees sent over from Louis Noisette, of Charleston, USA. She got together 250 species, thereby giving great impetus to the rose-growers of Lyons. As early as 1804 she said: 'In ten years time I want each department to possess some rare plants from my greenhouse.' And, indeed, she was to supply botanical gardens throughout the whole of France. In the meantime, she set up a model farm, reared pedigree cattle and extended her property to include the Beau Préau woods and the St Cucufa pond. This elegant and worldly woman proved herself to be a shrewd landowner.

It soon became obvious that the château was too small. Percier and Fontaine added on two wings and pulled down the dividing walls in order to enlarge the drawing rooms. In doing so they practically caused the main structure to collapse and had to reinforce it with massive pilasters which still today look somewhat incongruous. The interior was decorated with care in the taste of the day. The walls were hung with both antique and modern pictures. Two red marble obelisks adorned one of the doorways; they came originally from the Château de Rueil, once the residence of Cardinal de Richelieu but now non-existent. Berthault built follies in the shade of the trees; a Gothic aviary, a temple of love, sphinxes were dotted about the groves and the banks of the stream.

In this setting, which every month became more beautiful, bloomed a country-house life such as we still know today in England. Serious matters were dealt with amongst themselves and, apart from the diversions, Bonaparte put in long hours of work either in the library or else on the little bridge covered over with tent canvas which crossed the moat.

Except for feast days and ceremonies there were not many guests, but its proximity to Paris enabled Bonaparte to reach it on horseback in three quarters of an hour and to summon hastily ministers, generals or important visitors for a special interview.

From 1804 on, after the coronation, they were obliged to live at Fontainebleau, Compiègne or St Cloud, which were royal

The west façade, reinforced by Napoleon with pilasters to prevent the structure collapsing. The two obelisks are of red marble and came from Cardinal de Richelieu's nearby Château de Rueil

OPPOSITE: *An angle of one of the two wings added by Percier and Fontaine in 1799 to enlarge the original structure. It is shaded by the trees which Joséphine imported from many parts of the world*

RIGHT: *The far end of Napoleon's library, with the desk from Compiègne. The cupola above it is decorated with classical designs. When he divorced her in 1809, Joséphine left this room exactly as Napoleon had known it*

A detail of Joséphine's spinet in the Music Room, where much of the furniture was designed by Jacob

The mantelpiece in the Music Room

residences. Joséphine deplored this, since it meant missing the blooming of her most cherished flowers. In 1809 Napoleon decided to divorce. It was to Malmaison that the Empress retired, preserving as relics those objects which her husband had left there. She alone dusted his study where his papers remained just as he had left them.

It was from Malmaison, surrounded by her flowers, that she witnessed those splendours, of which she had seen the beginnings, crumble into ruin. The Allied armies invaded France, Joséphine fled, and then on the insistence of the Tsar and the King of Prussia she returned to her home. There she received the charming Alexander and entertained him with a touching unawareness – or was it perhaps with secret intent to soften the fate of the exiled Emperor? And then suddenly, on May 29, 1814, she died.

Napoleon heard the news at Elba. He returned twice to Malmaison during the Hundred Days. He had hardly set foot in France when he paid his first visit and he entered alone into Joséphine's deserted room and emerged, his eyes swollen with tears. The second was while he was still free and the Allies were deliberating his fate. For four tragic days he stayed there, seeking to escape the consequences of his final defeat, while Fouché urged him to abdicate for the second time. A few of the women he had loved came to be beside him, his stepdaughter Hortense, who surrounded him with affection, his mother, and some callers, Madame de Pellapra, Countess Walewska. From there

The mantelpiece in the Council Chamber, which takes the form of a tent made of striped silk

A bronze by Mouton of Napoleon measuring distances on a map, made in 1809

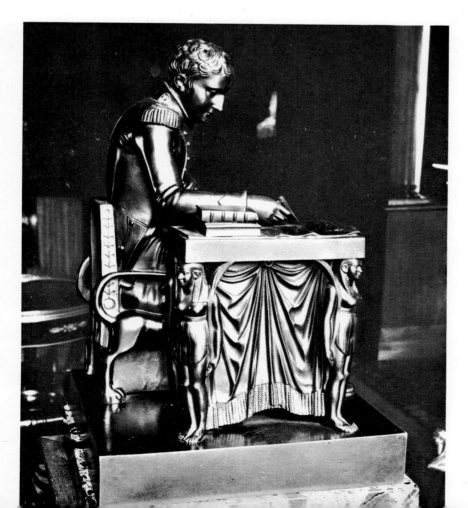

Malmaison was a place for relaxation, study and imperial politics

Joséphine de Beauharnais, a portrait by Gérard done at Malmaison in 1807. She bought Malmaison in 1799 while Napoleon was absent in Egypt, and continued to live there after their divorce in 1809 until her death in 1814. She is buried in the parish church at Rueil

LEFT: *A grisaille by Laffitte in the dining-room, and an epergne presented to Napoleon by the City of Paris*

LEFT: *Busts of the Emperor's family are arranged around the walls*

The harp in the Music Room, surmounted by the imperial eagle, signed by Cousineau

An octagonal table in the reception-room, with ormolu figures of the seasons by Thomire on the upper part

OPPOSITE: *The dining-room, one of the suite of rooms which were decorated in 1799 by Percier and Fontaine*

at last, after hours of anguish and hesitation, he left for Roche-fort, still hoping for an honourable exile.

The Tsar, who had become attached to all the Beauharnais, for whom he had shown much consideration, was touched by the grief of Eugène, Joséphine's son, and also by his financial plight. He did him the service of buying, forthwith, the collection of pictures, and so today they are to be found at the Hermitage Museum in Leningrad.

On the death of Eugène, Malmaison was sold and over a long period it passed through many hands. Louis XVIII and Charles X went there, however, to hunt in the woods on the estate. Bought back by Napoleon III, put up for auction again by the Third Republic it was finally acquired by M. Osiris, a philan-thropist and patron of the arts, who converted the château into a museum and presented it to the French State in 1904.

Throughout these vicissitudes, the grounds the Empress had lovingly planned had been divided for the most part into lots. Modern houses were built and are still being built, in what was once the park, and in many gardens one sees here a little temple, there a pair of sphinxes, the remains of Berthault's graceful crea-tions. The greenhouse no longer exists, but the pavilion against which it stood is still there.

And yet, reduced in size and surrounded as it is by encroach-ing suburbs, Malmaison still enjoys enough space and beautiful trees to give it the illusion of the country and of solitude.

De Garneray's watercolours enable us to recapture the atmo-sphere of this place extraordinarily well. The outside of the house is intact, down to the curious little antechamber in the form of a tent, made at the instigation of Napoleon in order to avoid enter-ing directly into the great hall from outside, and which actually he found very ugly.

Inside, the ground floor has been restored more or less as it was. The library with its mahogany panelling, the music room with its furniture by Jacob (rediscovered after much trouble by successive curators) and its Turkey red hangings, the dining-room with its silver-gilt service presented to the Emperor at the time of the coronation, are there with a thousand trinkets, busts, paintings, watercolours, engravings, costumes, porcelain which had belonged to the illustrious couple or evoked their memory. On the first floor Joséphine's room has also been restored. In this charming circular room, adorned with little gilded pillars, draped with amaranth Indian muslin, and flooded with sun-light, it is easy to imagine the shadow of the woman of whom Napoleon said: 'She has more grace and charm than anyone I have ever seen.'

JACQUELINE DE CHIMAY

Fontainebleau

A hunting lodge which saw four centuries of French history

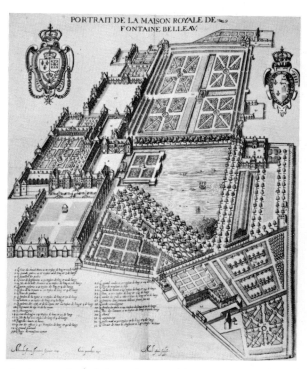

An impression of the palace and its gardens in *1614*. All the main elements were already completed by this date, including the four courts

THE HUGE AND MAGNIFICENT FOREST, the fresh water springs, its proximity to Paris, and its convenience as a halting place between the capital and the Loire valley, all pointed to Fontainebleau as the ideal site for the residence of a dynasty of kings passionately fond of hunting and obliged to make constant journeys round their domains.

Already in the twelfth century Louis VI, *le Gros*, built a dungeon there; then Louis VII erected a chapel which is believed to have been consecrated by Thomas à Becket as he fled from the wrath of his master, Henry II of England; St Louis founded a monastery to which Charles V, *le Sage*, added a 'library', and this group of buildings encircles the Cour Ovale.

But it was François I who made Fontainebleau into a true royal residence. Although from the outside the palace retained its severity – for the local sandstone lent itself less to delicate and florid sculpture than did the white stone from the region of the Loire – the decoration within was sumptuous. François, having built the great pavilion that looks on to the Basse Cour, the Golden Gate from which stretches a long, straight avenue right into the woods, and made the gallery which bears his name, called in Primaticcio from Bologna and Rosso from Florence who covered the walls with frescos, stucco and marble. He acquired works by Andrea del Sarto, Leonardo da Vinci, Raphael, Benvenuto Cellini, together with hundreds of other treasures, which in the course of time came to enrich the Louvre Museum. Infatuated with Italy, whose splendours had turned his head, he wanted Fontainebleau to become a 'second Rome'. The

OPPOSITE

ABOVE: *The château was altered in several different periods but still retains its unity*
BELOW: *The Cour du Cheval Blanc was built by François I between 1530 and 1540*

The east wing of the Cour de la Fontaine was also known as the Ancienne Comédie wing, since it contained the room in which plays were enacted

pleiad of artists which served this sovereign collector and patron of the arts was known as the 'First School of Fontainebleau'. Henri II completed the magnificent ballroom and made liberal use of his ambiguous cipher wherein the C of his wife's christian name, Catherine, when interlaced with his own H, curiously resembled the D of his mistress, Diane de Poitiers. Charles IX, whose name is so mournfully associated with the massacre of St Bartholomew, placed the plaster cast of a bronze horse in the Basse Cour which afterwards came to be known as the 'Cour du Cheval Blanc'.

Henri IV had a reputation for thrift, but he claimed that it was undeserved. 'They accuse me of being stingy,' he said, 'but I do three.things which are far removed from meanness – I make war, I make love, and I build.' Indeed, at Fontainebleau he doubled the size of the palace, laid out the design for the Jardin de l'Etang, constructed the long canal which flows towards Avon, and surrounded himself with French and Flemish artists, among whom were Fréminet, Ambroise Dubois and Toussaint Dubreuil. This was the Second School of Fontainebleau.

After this date the palace was never enlarged, but it underwent several alterations. We owe, together with other embellishments, the famous iron horseshoe staircase to Louis XIII and his architect Jean du Cerceau, and this was so successful that it served as a model and inspiration for a great many bad imitations.

The heart of Louis XIV, that great builder, was at Versailles, and in fact at Fontainebleau he showed a lack of discernment, and made the mistake of demolishing the 'Bains de François I' in order to make room for new apartments. He did, however, entrust the task of modernising the gardens to Le Nôtre, assisted by Le Vau (architect of Vaux-le-Vicomte). This was no easy matter since the façades of this palace with its many pavilions, and its disparate styles, were set in so many different directions. In his book *Le Nôtre* the Comte de Ganay explains how the symmetry was achieved by 'ingenious grouping of hornbeam hedges', how the irregular structure of the servants' quarters was disguised by 'clipping the trees in flat layers so as to conceal the line of the buildings', and how the difficulties involved in laying out the Great Flower Garden were overcome. Here it was not possible for Le Nôtre to work on a virgin landscape; the frame was already there and he had to adapt his designs accordingly. That he was able to do so is further proof of the genius of the incomparable gardener.

The influence of Louis XV, like that of his predecessor, was detrimental. He demolished the Galerie d'Ulysse, decorated by Primaticcio, an action much regretted and criticised at the time, as well as the Pavillon des Poêles dating from Henri II, and he

The Porte Dauphine was renamed the Baptistère when the future King, Louis XIII, was baptised in front of the gate in 1606

Looking across the Cour du Cheval Blanc to François I's wing. The construction of this wing was begun in 1528 by Gilles Le Breton

The horseshoe staircase at Fontainebleau inspired imitations throughout Europe

The famous horseshoe staircase was constructed by Jean du Cerceau for Louis XIII to replace Philibert Delorme's original staircase. It was used by Napoleon as a tribune when he took leave of his Guards in the Cour du Cheval Blanc after his abdication in 1814. Since then the courtyard has been known as the Cour des Adieux

70

BELOW: *A detail of the centre panel of one of the doors in the Throne Room*

replaced this with the Gros Pavillon employing Mansart as architect. Louis XVI converted the rooms formed by the angle of the courtyard into enchanting *petits appartements*, and he also enlarged the Galerie François I.

In 1793 the *sans-culottes* behaved here with greater restraint than at Versailles. 'The Revolution destroyed little', remarked Charles Terrasse, 'it robbed'. The treasures were saved, but the Emperor Napoleon found the palace devoid of furniture, a situation which he remedied. Of all the royal residences this was his favourite. Richer in history than Versailles ('It is a house belonging to the centuries,' he said) and yet less burdened with oppressive if glorious memories, it was here that he wished to live as Sovereign. The old walls and the forests rang once more with the joyful sounds of festivities and hunting. Arranged around the Bleau Fountain (or Bliaud or Belle eau) was the English Garden, perhaps inspired by that excellent gardener, the Empress Joséphine. One indication of the Emperor's interests was the establishment in part of the palace of the Military School which was later transferred to St Cyr. It was here also that Napoleon committed the most outrageously autocratic act of his reign by keeping Pope Pius VII prisoner for two years.

OPPOSITE: *The throne designed by Percier and made by Jacob for Napoleon. The Throne Room was the King's Bedroom from the time of Henri IV to Louis XVI, and was converted into a Throne Room by Napoleon*

A seventeenth-century engraving by Aveline showing the Cour de la Fontaine, the garden and the lake

OPPOSITE: *The Queen's Bedroom dates from the seventeenth century. The bed, made by the cabinet-maker Séné and decorated by Laurent and Hauré, belonged to Marie Antoinette. The chairs and the balustrade were made by Jacob and added to the room during the First Empire. Joséphine's jewel-chest is inlaid with mother-of-pearl and gilt bronze motifs*

Louis XVIII and Charles X went there but rarely. But Louis-Philippe, who was profoundly fascinated by everything the Emperor had liked, showed a lively interest in Fontainebleau. He over-restored Primaticcio's frescos to such an extent that Bernard Berenson cried: 'Primaticcio or not . . . it's dreadful!' But as a result of recent work these frescos can once again be seen in all their original freshness.

Thus almost all the French sovereigns left their mark on Fontainebleau. And with them lived their ministers, their architects, their courtesans, their queens, and a thousand ladies of times gone by whose ghosts return to haunt the visitor.

Here is Anne de Pisseleu, Duchesse d'Etampes, admiring the Mona Lisa which François I had just acquired. There is Diane de Poitiers who, they say, succeeded her in that King's affections and also seduced his son (and even his grandson?). Here is Gabrielle d'Estrées, the mistress of Henri IV; and Christina of Sweden who had her unfaithful lover, Monaldeschi, assassinated within these gilded walls, a deed which was considered to be in such bad taste that she was asked to leave the country. It was here too that the gentle Louise de la Vallière timidly succumbed to the passionate advances of the young Louis XIV. Some years later Madame de Maintenon watched him galloping back from

A doorway at the far end of the Gallery of François I

A detail of the Gallery of François I

the hunt along the avenue leading to the loggia by the Golden Gate where she awaited him, and there she persuaded him to revoke the Edict of Nantes, thereby condemning the French Huguenots to persecution and exile. There are shades also of Marie-Antoinette, happy in the intimate seclusion of the *petits appartements* and her Turkish boudoir – of Joséphine, sanguine in the bright, as yet untarnished glory of the Empire; and then of Marie-Louise, still fascinated by the extraordinary husband destiny had chosen for her.

And as one walks here one conjures up another picture – that of Napoleon bidding farewell to his guard in that Cour du Cheval Blanc which was henceforth known as the Cour des Adieux. And then, suddenly, there was Louis-Philippe, accompanied by his family, handsome young princes for whom the future must have seemed so brilliant. And finally with Napoleon III came the end of the pageantry. The Empress Eugénie would stroll with her ladies, in their crinolines and hoods, in the shade of the English Garden, and sometimes it amused her, as she came out of the Chinese Museum, to throw bread to the carp in the pond by the palace. How many events must these creatures, nearly three hundred years old, have unknowingly witnessed!

JACQUELINE DE CHIMAY

A relief of Henri IV by Jacquet, 1599

OPPOSITE: *The Salle des Gardes was almost entirely rebuilt in the reign of Louis-Philippe by Dubreuil and Moench. The parquet floor was made of fifteen different species of wood by Poncet*

Charlottenburg

The interior is a superb example of German decorative art

A wooden model of Schloss Charlottenburg showing the appearance of the Cour d'Honneur before the statue of the Great Elector was placed in the centre

THE RELATION OF SCHLOSS CHARLOTTENBURG to the now vanished Berlin Schloss and to Potsdam, is rather like that of the lost Whitehall Palace to Kensington and, say, Hampton Court. The Berlin Schloss with its Schlüter decorations was wantonly removed after the last war to make way for the Marx-Engels Platz in East Berlin; in Potsdam the Neues Palais and the Communs survive more or less intact, the Stadt Schloss and the Garnison church are ruined, while Sans Souci appears virtually as it ever did. Sans Souci was the idea and creation of a single monarch between 1745 and 1753. Charlottenburg has a longer history over a much greater span of years and indeed it might be said that its story still continues. From the Berlin Schloss down Unter den Linden through the Brandenburg Gate, the road runs straight along the Charlottenburger Chaussee past the Rondel of the Siegessäule to a fork at what is now the Ernst Reuterplatz where the proud cupola of Schloss Charlottenburg rises on the right at a distance of about eight kilometres in all.

The palace is set back in a park leading down to a bend in the Spree which borders one side of the gardens. Between the front courtyard and the main road there is a wide expanse of lawns separating the royal domain from the little town, which is now one of the better quarters of Berlin, with much the same attitude in its inhabitants as those of Kensington, and with just about as much justification. As it now stands the palace is an elongated complex stretching out on either side of the cupola court, combining several styles from high baroque to neo-classical rococo. The central portion with a rusticated base and pedimented

The garden front of the Schloss seen from the north-west. The central section including the cupola was designed by the Swedish architect Johann Friedrich Eosander in the first years of the eighteenth century

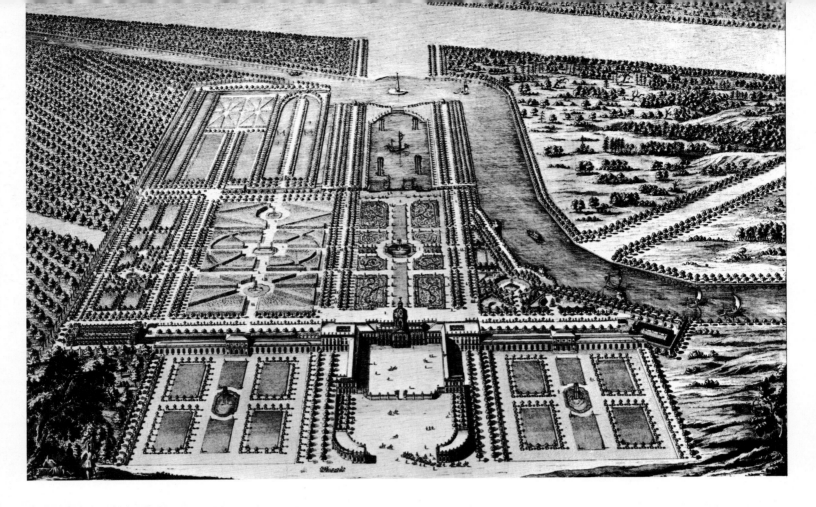

portico on the main front and an oval bay on the garden front is a small country house called Lützenburg which the Elector Friedrich III built for his second wife, Sophie Charlotte, the friend of Leibnitz, the philosopher, in 1695. The original architect was Arnold Nering, whose most famous building is the Berlin Zeughaus, but he died in the first year of building at Charlottenburg. As so often with German castles, the first project was no sooner under way that it was found to be insufficient, and the necessary wings, with quarters for the household and court, were soon found to be lacking.

In the meantime, Friedrich had become the first King of Prussia. He was crowned in 1701 in the Schlosskirche in Königsberg, specially decorated for the occasion by a Swede, Johann

Friedrich Eosander, later to be ennobled as von Goethe. It was this court architect who, after travels to Paris and possible consultations with Fischer von Erlach, was entrusted with the enlargement and aggrandisement of Lützenburg. The principal features of Eosander's additions were the imposing cupola (which, in spite of the long outside pavilion wings, still seems rather too high and top-heavy), the wings enclosing the *cour d'honneur*, and a wing to the left or west. He kept to the characteristics of Nering's block and the original structural features of yellow sandstone for the carved capitals and bases and brickwork covered with stucco. The colouring has remained until today in a deep yellow ochre, with slightly lighter touches in the carved sandstone. The works were being carried out with energy when Sophie Charlotte died suddenly in 1705, and the King changed the name from Lützenburg to Charlottenburg in her memory. All monarchs of the despotic enlightenment were avid builders and it is from this period that the cupola dates. At the very top the gilded figure of Fortuna swings in the wind. An apt invention for the story of Berlin and its buildings, yet even this vane was originally intended for Andreas Schlüter's ill-fated Mint Tower project (ill-fated because, being built on the shifting Berlin sand, it fell down). The constructions continued until 1712.

Friedrich I laid upon his son the duty of bringing his palaces to the 'fullest perfection'. But Friedrich Wilhelm I abandoned all work except on the Berlin Schloss. However, he gave instructions for Charlottenburg to be kept heated and roofed. The treaty of Charlottenburg with King George I was signed there in 1725, and in 1728 it was the scene of days of glittering splendour for the visit of August the Strong of Saxony. As soon as Frederick the Great came to the throne in 1740, he began to make plans as a philosopher and poet to counteract the philistine dictatorship of his father. He appointed Georg Wenzeslaus von Knobelsdorff, a friend from his Rheinsberg days, to build an east wing. He himself followed progress with the greatest impatience from his Silesian campaign, and arrived back from the war in 1742 to be greeted by a poem from Voltaire. The works continued until 1746. The greatest gem was the so-called Goldene Galerie, probably the greatest single work of the northern rococo. Friedrich Wilhelm II began alterations in the Frederician wing, in accordance with the tenets of his time. The changes were principally on the ground floor and included two rooms in the Etruscan style, but Frederick the Great's winter apartments at the front of the wing were also altered in a style with overtones of Louis XVI. One room with decorative grisaille wall-painting on the ground floor by Wilhem Hodler, which was covered over with wall-paper, is now restored on the floor above. A theatre was added at the extreme west end of the complex, and, in the grounds, a belvedere. Both of these were finally damaged in

The cupola from the south-east. The gilt statue of the goddess Fortuna is mounted above it and acts as a wind-vane

A careful reconstruction of a monument to German baroque taste

John Churchill, Duke of Marlborough, probably painted during his visit to Berlin in 1704, by an unknown artist. The picture now hangs in Schloss Charlottenburg

OPPOSITE
ABOVE: *The central hall overlooking the formal gardens*
BELOW: *The Eicherne Galerie, in the older part of the palace, with oak panelling by the English carver, Charles King, who was attached to the court in 1703*

A view into the Eicherne Galerie

RIGHT: *A bedroom in the east wing*

82

Figures at the base of the Great Elector's monument

The gladiator near the main gate is a copy of an eighteenth-century original

November 1943. In a single air-raid the central block and the Knobelsdorff wing were burnt out and the entire palace severely damaged – hurts so severe that restoration still continues.

Under Friedrich Wilhelm III two highly important additions by Karl Friedrich Schinkel were made, a small house or pavilion for the King's second and morganatic wife the Princess Liegnitz (Gräfin Auguste von Harrach). Unfortunately this monument to a king's mistress was burnt out, but the Doric Temple or Mausoleum built for his dead wife in 1810 remains. It contains the moving recumbent figures of Queen Luise by Gottfried Schadow and of the King himself by Rauch.

The story of the Schloss not only continues in the activity of skilful restoration, but in the concerts and art exhibitions which are held there. One of the most extraordinary additions to its splendours is Schlüter's greatest work, the bronze mounted statue of the Great Elector which stands in the fore-court. It used to stand on the Kurfürsten or Lange Brücke in front of the Berlin Schloss. Towards the end of the war it was dismantled and placed in canal barges. By a miracle it was saved for the west and from certain destruction, and re-erected where it now stands.

The exterior of the palace is not particularly striking when compared with some others, in fact its strength is in its simplicity. It is – or was – for its interior decoration that Charlottenburg had special claims to be something out of the ordinary. Much has survived, and that which has not has been recorded in a particularly remarkable way. During 1943 it was decided to have the decoration photographed in detail. A number of superb colour photographs were taken (including some at the

Berlin Schloss and at Potsdam). Permission was not given for general views, and such as were taken were taken from the tops of ladders while supposedly taking the details. In the event the views of the Goldene Galerie were taken on the afternoon before it was destroyed completely.

Of the rooms that remain in the older section the most striking is the suite containing the Eicherne Galerie. This oaken gallery on the ground floor is panelled from floor to ceiling in warm oak, enriched with pilasters, gilded capitals and bases and a finely carved chimney-piece. The carving on the door panels and surrounds is probably by an Englishman, Charles King, who was named court carver in 1703. He is thus a contemporary of Grinling Gibbons, but very different from him in style. This gallery is typical of the rather dark wooden decoration which reminds one of part of Kensington Palace, though it is all somewhat richer. As a whole, the Frederician wing was undoubtedly the most successful.

Of all the suites only the ante-room to the King's apartments survived the flames more or less intact, and this room has its own especial importance because it contains some of Johann August Nahl's earliest decoration. In passing it must be said that Nahl's designs were even more delicate in their drawing than in their execution – like some stage sets by Benois or Messel. Only in the imagination can one see the wing aglitter with candles (not one of the holders has survived from the period), with consoles and chimney-pieces covered with Meissen porcelain.

One of the most important features of Frederick's palaces was his advanced collection of paintings by Frenchmen like Lancret, Pater, Boucher and Watteau. Inspired by Pesne, Frederick was one of the first collectors of Watteau. Two of the most famous works at Charlottenburg were the Watteau *Embarquement pour Cythère* and the *Enseigne de Gersaint*. The latter hung in the concert room. A sabre cut through it was caused during the Austrian invasion in 1760. The entire collection has survived the ages fairly well, for in a recent exhibition it was possible to show over a hundred works while only about one hundred and fifty have been dispersed or destroyed. Books bound in red or green, either by Frederick or his friends, gave *éclat* to his library and antique objects and busts gave further evidence of his culture.

Charlottenburg still has many attractions to offer in the paintings which have been restored to it, in its gardens and lawns, and the park laid out by Lenné. In the bustle of modern Berlin, one can be thankful for this quiet among the hysterical energies and the flow of traffic outside. If it is still not quite so splendid as once it was, it has a certain liveliness, as the craftsmen and stuccateurs and wood-carvers work patiently with gold and silver leaf re-creating a splendour that it has not known for years.

NICOLAS POWELL

The statue of the Great Elector by Andreas Schlüter now stands in the forecourt at Charlottenburg

Linderhof

Ludwig II's flamboyant fantasy in the neo-baroque manner

ONE SHOULD APPROACH LINDERHOF in a mood of reverence and delight. It is essential to view it not as a madman's dream but as a piece of fairy-tale architecture in a setting surprising and yet amazingly appropriate. The eye which sees it as so much white icing fallen from a wedding cake at a sylvan picnic is not worthy of it. The cultural snobbery which dismisses it because of its overwhelming sympathy for a period other than its own, blinds its victims to merits which are intrinsic and valid. It is in indisputable little masterpiece, and, in the light of that, its debt to the France of *Louis Quatorze* becomes an irrelevance.

Of all Ludwig's projects it was the only one complete at the time of his death. Money had been poured out of his privy purse upon it. Ludwig II did not expect the state of Bavaria to build him castles and palaces, but only to give its support to the raising of the enormous loans which made such building possible. Actually the state would be the ultimate beneficiary. The age of mass visitation was approaching, when an architectural white elephant could prove a most valuable asset. But his ministers did not see it in that light. They saw only someone heading for bankruptcy, loth to perform his monarchial functions, and, at the same time, filled with dreams of a splendour on which only his own eyes and those of a few privileged intimates were to be permitted to rest.

Linderhof's perfection might suggest that it was planned to the last detail, but, in actual fact, like Topsy, 'it jest growed'. The eloquent façade, so extraordinarily effective against the hillside backcloth of rock and steeply-rising trees, was, if not an after-

King Ludwig II of Bavaria

OPPOSITE: *The main façade of Linderhof, with the large basin in front of the palace containing the gilded group of Flora and Nymphs*

LINDERHOF

A watercolour of Linderhof by H. Brening. The great lime tree, from which the palace acquired its name, is clearly seen to the right of the central fountain

The south garden rises in three terraces to a marble rotunda overlooking the palace. A view taken in winter

thought, at least a later development. The palace was built piecemeal. It began as an extension, of a single bedroom, to an existent hunting-lodge, and went on to include a combined study and dining-room with a horseshoe-shaped cabinet at each of its four corners. All this was framed in weatherboarding and joined to the Königshäuschen – later removed and re-erected nearby – by a stair and gallery.

It was only in 1874 that G. Dollman, who became private architect to the King in that year, was asked to enclose all this, and to create the palace as we now know it. The Hall of Mirrors and the two Gobelin Rooms were added, and the present highly elaborate façade came into being which, someone has said, makes the contrast between sophistication and nature one of Linderhof's chief attractions.

The mountain valley of Graswang, where Linderhof makes its unexpected appearance, had been a place of periodic enchantment to Ludwig as a boy. His father, Maximilian II, had frequently used the tiny hunting-box which stood on the land of a tithe-farm belonging to the monastery of Ettal. The place derived its name from the Linder family, who in turn derived theirs from an old lime tree – Linde – which Ludwig insisted should be left *in situ* when he laid out his gardens. He had come to the throne in 1864, and purchased the site in 1869 when he was twenty-three years of age.

Ludwig ordered the ground to be levelled that same year. Grandiose plans seethed at all times in the brain of Wagner's ecstatic patron. He has been vindicated in the eyes of posterity architecturally as well as musically; but it is a little hard not to smile at some of the more fanciful of his schemes and actual erections, such as the colossal Winter Garden on the roof of the Munich Residenz, with its artificial lake and its painted back-

A nineteenth-century view of Linderhof show-ing the arrival of a sleigh at the main entrance, drawn by six richly caparisoned horses

cloth of the Himalayas, a piece of extravagent capriciousness which confirms the suspicion that the King was far from posses-sing infallible taste and had in him – as well as many fine inspira-tions – a good deal of Hans Andersen's potentate, who could be more entranced by a mechanical nightingale than by a living one. The original project for Linderhof, for example, was a vast, courtyarded construction in the Byzantine style. It can be seen in a drawing by Dollman and looks, in its immensity, as though it would have needed supplementing by an artificial Bosphorus to do it justice. This idea for Linderhof was replaced by a pro-ject, equally grandiose, for a Bavarian Versailles, a project which materialised eventually at Herrenchiemsee. Finally, the nymphs and dryads in the surrounding woods, shaken by this time to the very core of their being, must have whispered in Ludwig's ear the three words, 'Le Petit Trianon', and the situation was saved.

But Kreisel is right. Although 'Ludwig's villa was intended to express something of the spirit of the Bourbons . . . externally the building has nothing whatever in common with French architecture of the late seventeenth century and the early eighteenth. It is unmistakably stamped by the eclecticism of the time when it was built, 1874.' Linderhof is a tour-de-force in flamboyant neo-baroque, but, like a much later edifice with a quite different history, the theatre at Wiesbaden, it manages to project a personal effluvia of its own in spite of every plagiarism.

It was Dollman's first excursion into the neo-baroque. He was already supervising work of a very different nature at Neu-schwanstein; now he was asked to create an exterior for rooms already existent and which were decorated in a late rococo fashion. His versatility was equal to the occasion. He had no doubts, no hesitations, and, just as his drawing of the Byzantine palace suggests a building with several centuries of caliphate

The Throne Room. The throne is virtually hidden beneath its canopy lined with ermine

history behind it, so Linderhof was the authentic magnificence of a pre-Diderot era.

In one respect Ludwig out-Heroded Herod. No Bourbon edifice has ever had a site as dramatically effective. Use has been made of two sides and the narrow floor of a valley-opening, fringed by forest and rockface, as a multiple-terraced arrangement of flower beds and fountains which, however formal, is yet acceptable in this remote spot. Karl von Effner was the designer of the grounds, but he followed detailed directions of the king. Linderhof faces the slope of the Linderbichl to the south. There is just room at the back, on the steep slope of the Hennenkopf, for a cascade of thirty-two marble steps with a Neptune fountain at their foot and a trellised rotunda at the top, corresponding to the rotunda in the south garden. On either side of the palace is a formalised *parterre*, divided into four sections and with a border of trimmed hornbeams. The south garden is the really dramatic one, rising in three terraces from the large basin immediately in front of and below the palace. In the middle of the pool is a gilded group of Flora and her nymphs by Wagmüller, from the centre of which springs a jet of water ninety feet high. On each terrace-landing are oblong beds with low box edgings, and one mounts, past the two reclining nymphs of cast metal, past the niche containing the larger than life-size bust of Marie Antoinette – echo of the innumerable Bourbon themes in the palace itself – to the marble rotunda which was to have held an Apollo until Ludwig changed his mind and decided that it was the goddess Venus who must stand there. She was – he directed Hautmann – to be modelled from the Venus in Watteau's *Embarquement pour Cythère*. Hautmann's other limestone statues in the gardens are preferred by some people to Wagmüller's metal figures, but the latter have a grace which is singularly pleasing.

The radiating sun on the ceiling of the entrance hall with two putti *holding the Bourbon motto*

Ludwig II's bedroom was redecorated in 1886 by Julius Hoffman who modelled it on the famous Reiche Zimmer in the Munich Residenz

From this round temple one can look down to the huge fountain basin and to the white palace beyond, and then up to the green woods rising behind. The effect is one of magic and grace, and only so much ostentation as even nature allows herself occasionally in a highly colourful sunset.

It has been suggested that it was not so much Dollman who was responsible for the exterior of Linderhof as Ferdinand Knab, an artist who worked for him and who made sketches for a projected chapel and theatre which never came into being. The main façade has been rebuked for being to eclectic and too exuberant. In the niches of the upper storey the allegorical figures by Bechler and Perron – Education, The Army, Jurisprudence and the Peasantry – are of classical descent, whereas Walker's *Victory*, in a central position above the entrance, has a baroque elation; very much in accord with the genii and putti on the entablement, and with the huge figure of Atlas, carrying the globe, balanced on the topmost point of the gable above the Bavarian royal arms and four more allegorical figures. The general effect of all this statuary, and of the pillared projection above the three rounded arches of the entrance portal with their wrought-iron lattice-work, is rhapsodic; but the four high windows of the upper storey stabilise and add dignity to all this eloquence and charm. The other façades strike a more restrained note, but have still a regal distinction.

The interior of Linderhof, with the exception of the bedchamber – enlarged in 1884 and redecorated in 1886, in the reign of Julius Hoffman, Dollman's successor, when it was modelled upon Cuvilliés' famous *Reiche Zimmer* in the Munich Residenz – is largely the work of Franz Seitz, one of Munich's leading figures in the arts and crafts. As *Hoftheaterdirektor* he

The delicately carved balustrade of the staircase

LINDERHOF

A detail of the ornate carvings

was responsible for designing scenery and costumes at the court theatre; in 1867 he had seen to the sumptuous decoration of the King's magnificent apartments in the Residenz; and it was he who, in 1870, designed the King's magnificent coaches and sleighs. The north rooms owe much of their decoration to Christian Jank, a scene painter who made designs for the ceilings, 1870–71; but the brilliantly drawn, unsigned, pen-and-ink sketches for the decoration of the walls were almost certainly the work of Seitz. Angelo Quaglio, Joseph de la Paix and Adolf Seder were others who had a hand in the interior. Seder designed a number of the bronzes and was particularly successful in applying the ideas of Seitz.

The king's bed-chamber is now the largest room in the palace and has an authentic *Roi Soleil* magnificence, with its heavily gilded and richly carved protective balustrade, and its white wainscoting and gold woodcarving. When Ludwig named Linderhof 'Meicost Ettal', it was a hidden anagram on '*L'état c'est moi*, and not merely a reference to the monastery of Ettal nearby, ground landlord to the original tithe-farm. But *L'état c'est moi* definitely referred to Louis XIV and not himself. Linderhof was to be the tribute of one lover of beauty to another greater predecessor, and a bronze equestrian statuette of Louis in the vestibule is only one of a very large number of allusions in paint and marble and bronze to the French court.

As Kreisel has pointed out, rococo was a living style in the art of Bavaria until far into the nineteenth century: there was no need for Ludwig's artists to draw on French models. But when the latter did influence them – in a female bronze figure on a girandole, or in the ceiling paintings and the use made of crayon portraits – the result could be delightful. In the dining-room, the magic table, which could be lowered to reappear with a complete dinner, and which allowed Ludwig to dine in absolute solitude if he wished, was a French eighteenth-century device; but the Hall of Mirrors, the most magnificent of all the rooms in the palace, had had numerous precedents in the German Schlossen of the same epoch. The audience-chamber, the two Gobelin Rooms, and the four horseshoe-shaped corner cabinets, the Rose, the Blue, the Mauve and the Yellow, strike a note of modesty by comparison; but their furnishings and mural decoration are gracious enough in their way to suggest Schönbrunn. Linderhof, an anachronism when it was built, is now a delightful and satisfying work of art in its own right. As for the Moorish Kiosk in the grounds, purchased at the Paris Exhibition in 1867, and the famous Grotto with its artificial stalagmites and stalactites, these are pieces of nonsense perhaps best forgotten in adjacency to so much genuine beauty both of nature and of human devisal.

MONK GIBBON

Sans Souci

The light-hearted summer-house of King Frederick the Great

IN 1744 FREDERICK THE GREAT gave instructions to build a vineyard of three terraces (only later increased to six) on the southern side of a shady and sandy little height in the woods above Potsdam. On the 13th of January 1745, a cabinet order was given that building materials were to be assembled because the King intended to build a *Lusthaus* there. By 1747 the King was able to use the east side of the little palace; the term 'east-wing' is rather too much for a villa which is only ten rooms across the entire front and with only a service passage behind them. The decoration of the rooms was only properly undertaken after 1753, the year in which Frederick's architect, George Wenzeslaus Freiherr von Knobelsdorff, died. In the miniature library one can still see a drawing in the King's own hand with the first sketch for the palace: on the north side a colonnade leading to an entrance, a rectangular entrance hall opening into an oval cupola hall, the right wing 'pour le roy' consisting of four rooms, an ante-room, music-room, study-bedroom, and library, and three more rooms on the west side 'pour les étrangers', one of whom was to be Voltaire. That was all, except that finally there were in fact four rooms on the west end, one of which was the *Blumenzimmer*, now sometimes called the *Voltairezimmer*.

Von Knobelsdorff fought in vain for two things. The first was that the palace must have a cellar floor, because of the dampness of the sand on which it was to be built. In this he was perfectly right, as the marquetry floor has suffered, as have the bases of the walls. The second and more important point was that the little Schloss must be properly seen from the bottom of the

The garden-front seen from the foot of the terraces, with a statue of Venus after J-B Pigalle

OPPOSITE: *Frederick the Great's bedroom was in the alcove beyond the Ionic pillars, and contains the winged chair in which he died in 1786. The nearer part of the room was his work-room*

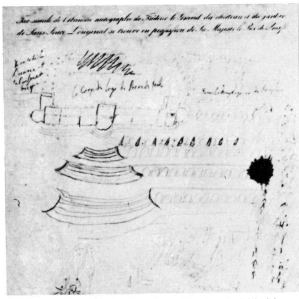

In 1745 Frederick the Great roughly sketched his ideas for the relationship of house to terraces, for the guidance of his architect, von Knobelsdorff. The sketch is preserved in the library at Sans Souci

The curving Corinthian colonnade flanking the entrance front by von Knobelsdorff

terraces, which cut into any distant view of it. This could have been achieved by reducing the width of the uppermost terrace, or by raising the whole pavilion on a slight plinth. Sans Souci has suffered from these two fundamental faults ever since.

The proudly careless words SANS SOUCI in bronze letters on the frieze above the front of the cupola room – like MON REPOS or DUNROAMIN over less famous villas – indicated the attitude of the King. His disregard for the appearance of this palace was deliberate. Sans Souci was to be an entirely private summer house above the vineyards, and Frederick intended to live an entirely private and unrepresentational life there. It is no secret that women were never entertained there during his lifetime. After all, the only woman he cared for was his sister, Wilhelmine Margravine of Bayreuth. And as for the necessary basement, it is likely that he decided to forgo this because of his impatience to make Sans Souci habitable as soon as possible, and it is not unlikely that he was anxious to have it finished, if not precisely on the cheap, at least with as little expense as possible. The summer-house character was underlined in the herms and caryatids which appear to hang from the architrave. They are so busy playing with grapes and twining roses that they have not much time for weight-carrying. The vine tendrils are symbolic of the situation of the palace above the glassed-in terraces of this northern vineyard. Whether von Knobelsdorff or Frederick had the first idea for the arrangement of the whole lay-out, the herms were certainly inspired by those by Permoser at the Dresden Zwinger, which Frederick had seen on a visit as Crown Prince.

One contrast is not without its point. The classicistic Corinthian colonnade faces a classical front typical of von Knobelsdorff, the designer of the Berlin opera house. The herm façade with the cupola bears the stamp of the soldier aesthete and the King who wished to have the music-room resound to his own flute concerts and his own compositions, when he was not engaged in teasing Algarotti or commissioning further tedious works from Graun or Quantz. The Frederican flutes in silver and ivory or amber inlays which are still to be seen in Sans Souci are almost as pathetic as the Beethoven ear-trumpets in Bonn.

The final pathos of Sans Souci, for those with any sense of history, is the winged chair in which the King died in 1786. He had a long reign, having come to the throne at the early age of twenty-eight. He was embittered, no doubt, by the brutality of his father, but he was a great general and the man who moulded the State of Prussia. His peaceful attributes should not be forgotten in an age when generals tend to be laughed at.

The entrance hall contains Corinthian columns exactly matching the colonnade outside. Doors lead off on the right to the service rooms, left to the corridor, and straight across to the cupola hall. Both halls were by von Knobelsdorff. The floor of the cupola hall was designed by Johann Christian Hoppenhaupt and executed in marble intarsia by Duquesnoy. The Italian marble blocks for this hall were too large to bring to Berlin, and two stone cutters, Heller and Grepler, were sent to Hamburg to work them in the rough. The most decorative room was without doubt the music room, with decorations by Johann Michael Hoppenhaupt and a series of wall paintings by the court painter, a Frenchman, Antoine Pesne, director of the Berlin Academy, who was here to be seen at his best. His series of gods and goddesses are far brighter and more cheerful than his usually rather insipid portraits of royalty and ballet dancers. The decoration is carried out quite simply in gold on white with trellis work leading across the ceiling to a spider's web in the centre. The most individual room is a little circular library with a doorway and bookcase let into a reddish cedar wood with light flourishes of chiselled and gilded bronze. The chasing is particularly delicate with thin flower garlands and implements and symbols of the arts by Johann Melchior Kambly. Oval bronze reliefs by Benjamin Giese are the only formal decoration. The floor is in a star design in light and brown-coloured woods centred on a rocaille marquetry flourish by J. H. Hülsmann. The Flower Room is quite different again. The general effect is citron yellow from floor to ceiling with an imposing Meissen chandelier. It was completed between 1752 and 1753 by J. A. Hoppenhaupt the Younger, with life-size cranes and little squirrels and monkeys and birds in full colour and relief amongst fruit and flowers. The flower swags appear to swing across the room and into the ceiling, while parrots are suspended in hoops in the spaces between the panels. Even the Kleine Galerie at the back of the main rooms has painted over the doors classical ruins rendered in red chalk surrounded by green pines and cypresses. The only room which is not stylistically *en suite* with the remainder is the study-bedroom of the King, designed by Friedrich Wilhelm von Erdmannsdorf in the year of the King's death in that room in 1786. It is more severely classical than the remainder and somewhat more modern and cold – in what we would loosely call a regency style. The bed alcove is divided from the larger part by

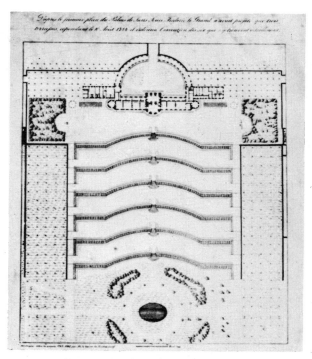

A plan of the terraces and original ground-plan of the house as envisaged by Jean Cabanis in 1744. At the top is the semi-circle of the entrance colonnade, and below the six terraces of the main garden, curved like shallow brackets

An eighteenth-century view of the Picture Gallery, which flanks the main house. It was designed by Johann Gottfried Büring and completed in 1764. It still survives today

The favourite palace of a Prussian King with French tastes

A contemporary view of the entrance courtyard

The Voltaire room decorated by J. A. Hoppenhaupt the Younger. The brilliance of the rococo is unequalled anywhere in Europe

RIGHT: *One of the two entrance halls, where pairs of marble columns and classical statuary create the impression of a king's sumptuous domain, gives no clue to the astounding rococo beyond*

A circular colonnade between Sans Souci and the Neues Palais

RIGHT AND BELOW: *Two views of the Chinese Pavilion built by Johann G. Büring in 1754–6. The figures of Chinamen are by Benkert and Heymuller*

two Ionic columns. It contains the famous winged armchair, but as well one of the most beautiful pieces of French eighteenth-century furniture, the King's writing-table, comparable only with Louis XV's desk at Versailles. The classical von Erdmannsdorf had visited England from 1764 to 1765, and was indeed an architect of a coming age who built the splendid but severe Schloss Wörlitz, and worked at Dessau.

Potsdam by no means consists of Sans Souci only. Two dependent constructions lie off the general axis of the grand allée, the so-called 'new rooms' and the picture gallery. The central and more representative building is the Neues Palais (1763–9), which is to be distinguished from the Marmorpalais and the Stadtpalais (now destroyed). Further buildings, added in the Romantic age, were the Roman Baths, the large Orangerie, the romanesque Fasanerie and the Friedenskirche of 1845–9.

The whole complex covers a vast acreage. There is a dragon temple (a pagoda copied from that at Kew by Chambers), temples of friendship, and belvederes, but one small building is so delightful that it cannot be passed over without comment. The Chinese Pavilion was built by Johann Gottfried Büring between 1754 and 1756. From a distance it looks a little like a round lodge with a steeply pitched roof surmounted by a little cupola. There is a simple frieze with a guilloche design and between each window there stands an enchanting figure. A sitting mandarin with a sunshade surmounts the whole. A four-columned portico on each front has two groups of seated figures: one with a tea ceremony and one of girls being offered by way of encouragement a taste of pineapples or mangoes. The columns are in fact gilded palm trees (as at Veitshöchheim or the confessionals at Zwiefalten). The figures are by Benkerl and Heymüller.

There was no lack of talent among the individual pieces of statuary in the park. *Mercury* and *Venus*, by Pigalle, were sent as gifts from Louis XV. There was also *Air* and *Water* by Lambert-Sigisbert Adam, and larger and highly competent groups by Glume, in the 1750's, in the best northern rococo style. These include the *Muses* rondelle and the so-called *Rondelle of the Rape* with a fine *Bacchus and Ariadne*.

It must be admitted that present guardians of Potsdam keep Sans Souci and the Neues Palais in reasonable repair, and the orderly crowds are not treated to too much dialectic materialism amongst their history, though the ghost of Frederick must thump with his cane and snort from time to time, for of all the owners of Potsdam (his father and the kings and emperors after him) it is his character which is most firmly stamped on Potsdam. Here more than anywhere else that strange and not entirely unsympathetic king seems to be immortal.

NICOLAS POWELL

Two laughing herms and a caryatid, part of the jovial group which extends across the whole width of the south front

OPPOSITE: *The figure representing Architecture below the cupola in the entrance hall. This 'Kuppelsaal' was designed by Hoppenhaupt and executed by Duquesnoy*

The Quirinal

The most venerable of the palaces in this city of palaces

The Horsetamers in the Piazza di Montecavallo

OPPOSITE

ABOVE: *An exterior view of the Quirinal and the piazza by Gaspare Vanvitelli*
BELOW: *Cardinal Barberini returning to the Quirinal in 1702 from a mission to Naples*

THE IMMENSE COMPLEX of the Quirinal Palace was the summer residence of the Popes until 1870 when it was seized by Vittorio Emmanuele. He died there in 1878 after receiving a message of pardon from the Pontiff he had outraged. The palace remained the home of the kings of Italy until 1946 and is now occupied by the President of the Italian Republic. Although the Savoyards endeavoured to remove the traces of the former occupants of the Quirinal, replacing the papal arms wherever possible with their own, the palace is essentially a monument to the taste of its builders, Gregory XIII, Sixtus V, Paul V and, to a lesser degree, Alexander VII and Clement XII. With its great irregular piazza it is among the noblest examples of that union of the baroque and the antique upon which the character of Rome so largely depends.

The piazza is dominated by the colossal marble statue of the Horse-tamers, grouped with an obelisk and a fountain to the right of the palace to close the long vista from the Porta Pia. The figures had been found in the ruins of the Baths of Constantine and stood on a low awkward base, together with other fragments, at the end of the Salita di San Silvestro, whence they gave the whole district its name of Montecavallo. Sixtus V ordered that the magnificent horses should be restored by the sculptors Flamini, Vacca, Leonardo Sormani and Pier Paolo Olivieri, and the statues were moved to their present position by Domenico Fontana. Inscriptions on their bases read *Opus Phidiae* and *Opus Praxiteles*, but the sculptures are considered to be copies of Greek originals. The red granite obelisk now rising between the

CLEMENTE XI PON·M·SEDENTE
CAROLVS PRIOR PRESBYTERORVM S R E. CARDINALIS BARBERINVS DE LATERE LEGATVS
AD PHILIPPVM V·HISPANIARVM REGEM CATHOLICVM, NEAPOLIM APPVLSVM, EXPLETO
FELICITER TANTO MVNERE SIBI BENIGNISSIME DE MANDATO ANNO ÆTATIS SVÆ SEPTVAGESIMO TERTIO
IAM INCHOATO, SOSPES VRBEMINGREDITVR, AC SOLEMNI DE MORE EQVITATV CONTENDIT ADPALATIVM
APOSTOLICVM QVIRINALIS, COMMISSÆ PROVINCIÆ RATIONEM TANTO PONTIFICI EXPLICATVRVS
❧ DIE XX IVLY   M DCCII ❧

The façade of the Quirinal looking onto the Piazza di Montecavallo was designed by Carlo Maderno and Domenico Fontana in 1589. The statues of the Horse-tamers were found in the ruins of the Baths of Constantine and were set up in their present position during the reign of Pope Sixtus V

two horse-tamers was brought to Rome from Egypt by Claudius in AD 57 and placed at the entrance to the Mausoleum of Augustus. It was set up in the Quirinal Piazza by Antinori for Pius VI in 1781. The basin, found in the Forum Romanum became part of the monument in 1818.

The Quirinal hill is but a slight eminence, yet it commands one of the finest views of the city; and although it is less than a mile distant from the Vatican it does not seem strange that Gregory XIII should have chosen it as the site of his summer retreat, for in the hot season the air is noticeably cooler here. During the years 1572 and 1573 the Pope paid frequent visits to Ippolito d'Este who rented his splendid villa on the Quirinal from the Neapolitan family of the Caraffa. Gregory was so enchanted by the locality that he at once formed a plan to build on the hill. But it was not until ten years later, in May 1583, that he commissioned Ottaviano Mascherino to erect a palace on the estate of the Cardinal d'Este. By the autumn of 1584 all the north part of the great house with its loggia and beautiful shallow spiral staircases was ready to receive the Pope.

The property and land on which the palace stood still belonged to the Caraffa although it was leased to Ippolito d'Este. When the Cardinal died in 1586, Gregory's successor, Sixtus V, immediately set about obtaining possession of the whole estate. The purchase was completed in 1587 and Sixtus then turned his attention to the enlargement of the building. Domenico Fontana re-designed the piazza, built the façade and together with Carlo Maderno planned the huge front and massive doorway giving onto the via Pia.

When Sixtus died at the Quirinal in August 1590, the palace was still unfinished and it was left to Paul V to bring the work of his predecessors to a conclusion. During the hot Roman

OPPOSITE: *The library is one of the best preserved examples of Pietro Piffetti's art. The floor, walls and ceiling are inlaid with elaborate arabesques and figure compositions engraved on ivory and mother-of-pearl*

The Sala Regia was designed by Carlo Maderno for Pope Paul V in the early seventeenth century. Two statues by Berthelot and Bernini support the papal coat-of-arms above a relief of Christ washing St Peter's feet by Taddeo Landini. The painted decoration was designed and carried out under the direction of Agostino Tassi in 1611–17

summers when the Vatican was exposed to malaria he passed more and more time at the Quirinal and he therefore decided to extend it still further, adding a spacious chapel suitable for the celebration of all the greater solemnities, a private chapel and the grand room known as the Sala Regia. He employed the most famous artists of the day to decorate these and the principal apartments of the palace. Two small churches and many houses had to be demolished to make way for Paul V's ambitious schemes. The work went rapidly forward until by 1618 he at last considered his residence worthy of a sovereign whose dominion spread over the whole world.

The direction of the work was entrusted first to Flaminio Ponzio and, after his early death, to Carlo Maderno. Ponzio planned the Pope's private chapel, the Cappella dell' Annunciata, in the form of a Greek cross, in 1610, and he was also responsible for the design of the main staircase and of the portal facing the piazza, completed, according to its inscription, in 1618. Two free-standing columns of cipollin marble support a broken pediment, upon the curves of which recline the haloed figures of St Peter and St Paul sculpted by Guillaume Berthelot and Stefano Maderno. Between them stood the charming little *Madonna and Child* by Pompeo Ferrucei, now filling the open pediment above the benediction loggia added later by Bernini.

Ponzio's severe and imposing staircase consists of two flights advancing to meet one another between panelled stone walls. The landing where they converge is adorned by an important fresco by that rare fifteenth-century master, Melozzo da Forli. It is a picture of God the Father surrounded by angels. The awe-inspiring majesty of the subject, and the gravity of the full, austere forms, are conveyed with moving simplicity and directness of feeling bred of an age which had passed more than a century before the Quirinal was built. The fresco was originally commissioned by Cardinal Riario, nephew of Pope Sixtus IV, for a chapel in SS Apostoli, Rome, and was only brought to the palace in 1711 when the church was rebuilt.

The difference in temper which separates Melozzo's painting from the works of the seventeenth century is strikingly illustrated by Guido Reni's interpretation of the same subject in the Cappella dell' Annunciata. Instead of confronting a static composition instinct with the aloofness of the god-head, the spectator is drawn into a conflux of ecstatic beings and invited to participate in their emotion. Reni was recommended for the work of decorating the chapel by his patron, Cardinal Scipione Borghese, who was at the same time the Pope's nephew. Paul's anxiety to see the work finished forced the painter to seek assistance, and some of the frescoes are by his friends Lanfranco, Albani, Antonio Carracci, Jacopo Cavedoni and the less distinguished Tommaso Campano. Guido's own glowing work in this little oratory includes not only the altarpiece of the Annunciation and the fresco already mentioned, but the very original, *genre*-like lunette scenes of the life of the Virgin.

The Sala Regia and the adjoining Cappella Paolina were both designed by Carlo Maderno. The richly gilded ceiling of the Sala Regia displays the arms of the Borghese Pope, and the heraldic devices of his house, the dragon and the eagle, mingle with arabesques and full-blown flowers to fill heavy coffers of irregular shape. They make a geometric pattern which is doubly repeated by the floor, once by the design of the rose, cream and grey inlaid marbles and again by the reflection in the shining surface. Round the walls runs a deep, painted frieze, one of the most surprising works of the period, designed and executed under the supervision of Agostino Tassi, best known as the master of Claude, but revealed at the Quirinal, not only in this room but also in the Stanza di San Paolo and the Stanza del Diluvio, as a superb painter of illusionist perspective as well as of poetic landscapes. The Sala Regia frieze shows arches and vistas

The entrance portal, designed by Flaminio Ponzio in 1618. The balcony was added later by Bernini

The entrance courtyard, except for the chapel, was the work of Flaminio Ponzio. A member of the President's Guard stands in the colonnade

The seventeenth and eighteenth centuries contrasted

The eighteenth-century Sala dei Parati Genovesi. The walls are covered with appliqué work on silk

OPPOSITE: *The Cappella Paolina was designed by Carlo Maderno and decorated by Martino Ferabosco*

opening into imaginary rooms with figures leaning out from balconies. The figures are by Lanfranco and Carlo Saraceni.

The long narrow chapel is approached beneath a relief in white marble of Christ washing St Peter's feet by Taddeo Landini. The walls are covered with pale illusionist paintings of columns, niches and statues, but it is the gilded stucco ceiling, the work of Martino Ferabosco, which gives this interior its splendid aspect. Religious subjects alternate with the arms of Paul V, in the centre an angel flies across an ornamental cross bearing a monstrance and round the edge of the vault Paul's chief constructions are depicted in gold relief.

Later in the seventeenth century, in 1657, the Quirinal was again the scene of a great work of collaboration, directed this time by Pietro da Cortona who was commissioned by Alexander VII to decorate the apartment known after the Pope as the Galleria di Alessandro. Salvator Rosa, Grimaldi and Mola were painting side by side here with Carlo Maratta, Guglielmo Cortese, Giovanni Pàolo Schor, Filippo Lauri and Lazzaro Baldi. Mola's *Joseph and his Brethren*, a romantic composition of figures, a classical palace and an idyllic landscape, is his masterpiece.

In other of the extensive apartments of the palace, reminders of ancient Rome, antique busts and delightful mosaics of birds, animals and butterflies have been brought into harmony with seventeenth- and eighteenth-century marbles and furnishings. The eighteenth century is represented by three major works, the mirror room in the Chinese style, completely hung with appliqué designs on cream-coloured silk, the Coffee House by Ferdinando Fuga, and one of the best preserved examples of the intricate art of Pietro Piffetti, a miniature library, the floor, ceiling and walls of which are all inlaid with elaborate arabesques, flowers,

A detail of the painted frieze along the walls of the Sala Regia, designed by Agostino Tassi, 1611–17. The figures leaning from the carpet-hung balconies are the work of Giovanni Lanfranco and Carlo Saraceni

shells, dancing amorini, maps and figure compositions engraved on ivory and mother-of-pearl. A remarkable bureau by Piffetti, entirely covered with inlay work, was brought to the Quirinal by Vittorio Emmanuele from Turin.

The Coffee House is a plain little classical building in the English style, embellished with frescoes by Panini, Battoni, Jan van Bloemen and Placido Costanzi. It is but one of the features of the formal gardens where palms, orange trees, statues, *terme* and fountains enliven squares of green enclosed by clipped box hedges in the stiff manner which seems to belong especially to Rome. The gardens owe their present appearance chiefly to Paul V. Evelyn visited them in 1644 and found them much as they look today. He was enchanted by the oddity of some of the water devices, the most extraordinary of which, an organ played by water, still exists.

OLIVE COOK

The spiral staircase was designed by Mascherino for Pope Gregory XIII and completed in 1584

The Royal Palace
NAPLES

A majestic situation for the palace of a vanished kingdom

The entrance façade of the Royal Palace on the Piazza Plebiscito was designed by Domenico Fontana and completed in 1602. Fontana was also the architect of the Quirinal Palace in Rome

THE FAÇADE OF THE Quirinal Palace, Rome, and that of the Royal Palace at Naples are both the work of Domenico Fontana. Both are three-storey buildings with a strong horizontal emphasis. But here the resemblance ends, and few people would spontaneously attribute these two elevations to the same author. The facts that the portal of the Quirinal was added later by other hands and that the ground floor at Naples was disfigured by grotesque statues in the nineteenth century have little bearing on this reaction: it is conditioned by the overwhelming effect of the colour of the Naples palace. Fontana, a newcomer to the southern capital, seems to have abandoned himself to the Neapolitan love of colour with even more fervour than the local architects. The palace is a startling composition of grey granite quoins and frames against brilliant Pompeian red walls, flaming along one side of the wide Piazza Plebiscito and glowing above the palms in a public garden towards the sea.

Fontana, who had made a name for himself in Rome not only as an architect but for his great engineering feats, fell into disfavour after the death of his patron, Sixtus V, and from 1592 made Naples his home. He was appointed 'Royal Engineer' under the Spanish Viceroys and the palace was the most important of the many works carried out under his direction. It was begun under Count Lemos in 1600. The façade was finished by 1602 but the rest of the building was not completed until 1730, more than a century after Fontana's death, although his plans were closely followed throughout.

When Charles III of Bourbon came to the throne in 1734, he

ABOVE: *The central section in a bird's-eye view of Naples in the seventeenth century. The most prominent buildings surrounding the harbour are* (from left to right) *the Castel dell'Ovo* (with flag) *which dates from 1154; the Royal Palace* (centre); *and the turreted Castel Nuovo, built in 1279*

LEFT: *The façade facing the Bay of Naples, painted Pompeian red with green shutters. It was built to the design of Domenico Fontana but not completed until 1730, more than a century after his death*

THE ROYAL PALACE, NAPLES

The entrance façade. The statues representing the rulers of the kingdom of Naples, from Roger the Norman to Vittorio Emmanuele, were added during the reign of Umberto in 1887–88

BELOW: *The palace in 1727, from J. B. Homann's plan of Naples, printed in Nuremberg. The garden in in the foreground runs down to the water's edge*

at once set about extending the palace. He added the wing along the sea front to house his remarkable collection of incunabula and manuscripts, which formed the nucleus of the present National Library, and commissioned G. A. Medrano to design an opera house. The famous San Carlo Theatre was completed in one year, 1737, an elegant structure adorned with reliefs of Apollo, Orpheus, and the Muses crowning Sophocles and Euripides, built of the same grey stone as the palace, but coloured white and pale ochre in pronounced contrast to the red of the adjacent palace. Fuga and G. M. Bibiena contributed later to the horseshoe-shaped interior, and the atrium and porticoes in front of the façade were the work of Antonio Niccolini in 1812. This same architect restored the theatre after it had been severely damaged by fire in 1816.

During the reign of Ferdinand II, between 1837 and 1842, many of the royal apartments were redecorated by G. Genovesi. He was responsible for the present aspect of the vast double-

flighted staircase of palest grey, white and pink marble. Fontana's design, carried out by F. A. Picchiati in 1651, still governs its noble sweep and stupendous proportions, but the vitality of its movement has been quenched by Genovesi's treatment of the balustrade, by the great chill white figures he has set in the wall niches and by his ceiling decoration of flaccid winged beings enclosed in garlands of laurel.

Pelagio Palagi also worked for Ferdinand II. Some of the richest gilt stucco work is his and among the few pieces of furniture still to be seen in the palace is a set of gilt bronze chairs which are typical examples of his fantasy. The legs and arms take the form of winged maidens. Palagi's work links Naples with Turin, where he was intensively employed; and the two palaces were more closely connected when Vittorio Emmanuele became King of Italy. He entered Naples on November 7, 1860 and on the following day he was invested with the sovereignty of Naples and Sicily in the Throne Room of Francis II, the last of the

Two magnificent rooms decorated in the eighteenth century

One of the rooms decorated for Ferdinand I and IV and Maria Carolina. The portrait is of the Archduchess Maria Josepha by G. Doyen

LEFT: *The Gallery. The ceiling is painted with scenes of historical events during the two centuries of Spanish rule in Naples*

A view from the Throne Room looking through the series of state reception rooms towards the entrance. The windows overlook the Bay of Naples. The rich marble of the floor was quarried in Apulia, and the grey marble surrounds of the doors are repeated throughout the palace

OPPOSITE: *The Throne Room, which was redecorated in 1837–42 for Ferdinand II by G. Genovesi. The gilt stucco figures around the frieze symbolise the provinces of the kingdom of Naples. It was in this room that Vittorio Emmanuele was invested with the sovereignty of Naples and Sicily after the unification of Italy*

Bourbons. The gilded throne with its lion arms still stands on its dais beneath a canopy of crimson velvet and patterned brocade. On the broad frieze above it boldly modelled gilt-stucco female figures symbolise the provinces of the Kingdom of Naples and immense trophies of arms gleam against a background of green and white, casting a gold reflection across the smooth marble floor divided by thick bands of white into hexagons of mulberry red and sage green. It is a sumptuous but, despite its voluptuous colouring, a sombre room.

There is indeed a sultry undercurrent in the whole atmosphere of this richly dark and ornate interior. The long panels of doors set in bottle-green frames show rococo scrolls, fruit, flowers and maidens balancing baskets on their heads against a gold background, a gigantic mirror flings back the light from two tall windows, but the glitter is instantly absorbed by brocaded walls of so deep a crimson as to appear almost black. The daring geometric patterns of the marble floors, flaunting red and green diamond shapes bordered by yellow on a white ground, squares of vivid orange and purple edged by grey-green, lozenges of pink in a plum-blue setting or white strap-work on rose and gold; the subtle hues of silks and brocades from San Leucia, intense blue, lilac, rust red and moss brown; the most inventive ceiling stuccos, white on gold, gold on white, all fail to dispel the settled gloom of these apartments.

It is encouraged by the large number of prominent pictures by followers of Caravaggio and painters of the Neapolitan school hanging on the walls. Mattia Preti, Honthorst, Andrea Vaccaro, Jan Lys, the gifted and prolific Luca Giordano and Solimena are all represented by memorable, restless works in which sable shadows are dramatically pierced by a lurid shaft or point of light. These haunting canvases completely efface the impression made by pastoral panels depicting incidents in the life of Don Quixote or of the battle frescoes dating from the time of the Spanish Viceroys on the barrel vault of the long gallery next to the Throne Room.

The Savoyards left a memento of their ownership of the palace which certainly adds to the feeling of melancholy and disquiet it arouses: Umberto adorned Fontana's façade with the statues already mentioned. They are costume figures of colossal size representing the rulers of the Two Sicilies, beginning with Roger the Norman and ending with Vittorio Emmanuele, sculpted in white marble. They were all carved in 1887 and 1888 and are indistinguishable in style although each bears a different signature: Raffaelli Belliazzi, Gemito, Ameridola, Solari, Franchesi, Cadegiano. They ruin the dignity of the elevation and give a comic opera twist to the building which is totally at variance with its purpose.

OLIVE COOK

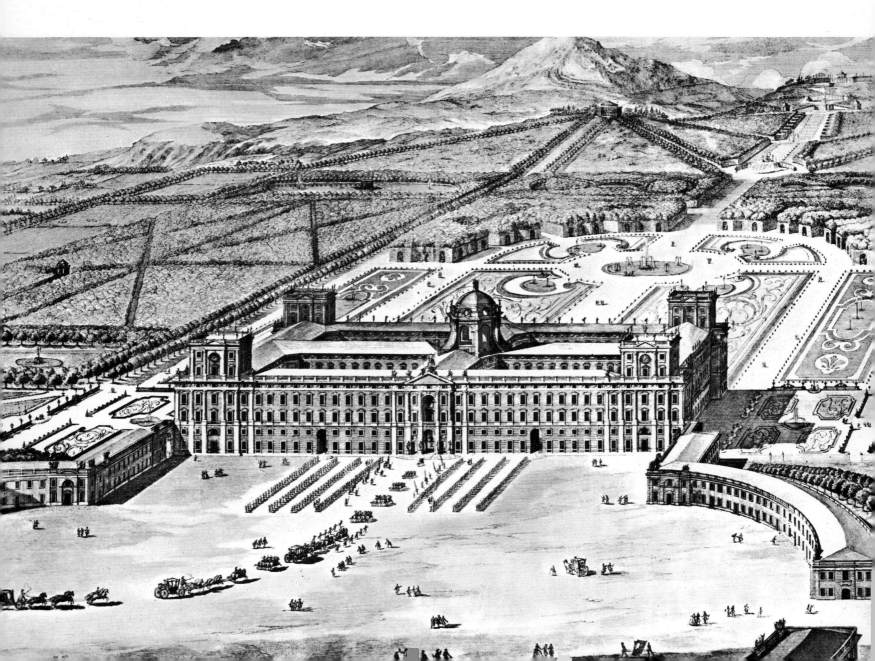

Caserta

The monumental scale of a palace executed for the Bourbons

THE PALACE AT CASERTA was designed as the central feature of a vast landscape; it was to have been the goal of an avenue of plane trees some sixteen miles long leading directly from Naples to the royal residence, a straight line which would have been extended a further two miles by the great ribbon garden behind the house. Although the avenue scarcely runs beyond the confines of the town and although the glass and concrete blocks of recent years rise cliff-like in the neighbouring streets and countryside, the palace still dwarfs everything in the whole wide plain between Monte Virgo and the sea.

It is no surprise to discover that it was the work of slaves, of prisoners captured by the royal navies on the shore of Tripolitania and of criminals from the *bagnios*. Intended as the summer residence of the Bourbons, it sprang into being at the command of Charles III, son of Philip V of Spain, who had succeeded the Austrian Viceroys as ruler of the Two Sicilies in 1734. The palace had risen only as far as the first storey when, in 1759, Charles was proclaimed King of Spain and had to leave Naples, making over the kingdom to his third son Ferdinand under the regency of the minister Tanucci. The work went on through the reigns of Ferdinand and Francis I and the decoration of the state rooms was completed by Joachim Murat and Ferdinand II.

The architect chosen by Charles to plan and execute his project was Luigi Vanvitelli who was born in Naples in 1700, the son of a painter from Utrecht. Luigi numbered Pope Clement XII among his patrons and was already recognised as an architect of distinction. Charles III himself laid the foundation stone

The enormous proportions of the marble staircase

OPPOSITE

ABOVE: *The entrance façade of the Palace of Caserta*
BELOW: *An eighteenth-century drawing showing how Caserta would have looked if the four corner towers and central cupola had been built*

of the palace on January 20, 1752 and Vanvitelli was still at work on it when he died in 1773. His son Carlo finally brought the exterior to a conclusion, though not entirely according to the original plans, which can be studied not only in a volume of engravings published by the architect in 1756 but in a long shallow room at Caserta where they are preserved together with a white marble statue of Vanvitelli in the dress of his period. The drawings show four corner towers and a central dome which were never realised.

They could hardly have enhanced the overwhelming effect of the palace. The extravagant scale of the peach, ochre and crimson façade seen at close quarters confirms the impression made by the building from a distance. But the stupendous dimensions are at first the only indication that the composition has anything in common with the flaming baroque fantasies of its period. It is absolutely geometrical, logical, austere and massively immobile. The long monotonous front is framed by slightly projecting pillared pavilions at either end, and in the centre a powerful pediment, neither broken nor open, surmounts two simple arches, one above the other. No sooner, however, does the visitor gain the entrance than any sensation of rigidity, any hint of outworn classicism, vanishes. He finds himself in a monumental vestibule of prodigious length cutting right through the width of the building and commanding a telescopic vista of a cascade falling in two snow-white zigzags against a leafy background.

One of the cross-section drawings made by Vanvitelli, showing the original plan for a central cupola and two of the four corner towers

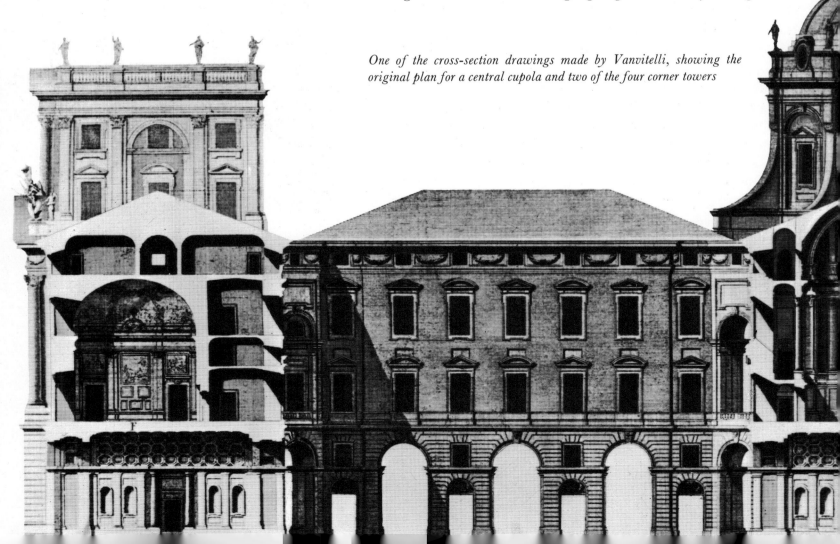

And now the vestibule is seen to move in a stately rhythm controlled by three octagons, one at each end and one in the centre, where lofty arches and great marble Ionic columns form into unexpected diagonals, yielding receding views into four courtyards. The enormous proportions reduce the human figure to pygmy insignificance and create a well-known nightmare atmosphere which is intensified as the majestic staircase comes into sight, ascending at right angles to the central octagon. It is all of pink and grey marble of a salty pallor as though the sea had but just ebbed from the mighty steps. These glide regally up to a broad landing where two realistic marble lions, the work of Tommaso Solari and Paolo Persico, snarl at the intruder, then divide into two flights turning in sharp countermotion along the walls towards a screen of three arches and an upper octagon and ambulatory immediately over the one below. Fabulous arched prospects open out on every hand, merging into one another, mysteriously expanding and contracting as the beholder crosses the shimmering floor of inlaid marbles towards the ponderous doors opening into the chapel (under repair from damage during the Second World War) and into the royal apartments.

The first of these, the Halberdiers' Hall, echoes the mood of the staircase. Its exquisitely blanched lilac and grey marbles appear to be salt-encrusted; the soaring vault, the Ionic pilasters, the white stucco reliefs and the titanic sculpture of Victory crowning Alexander Farnese, carved out of a column from the

The original layout of the palace and gardens, showing the intended piazza in front of the palace

The balustrade and statues above the cascade of Aeolus

Temple of Peace in Rome, all fulfil the expectations aroused by the noble entrance. But none of the other apartments exhibits the daring architectural imagination of the vestibule and staircase. The size and extent of the interior does indeed intimidate and amaze the visitor. As he wanders through the endless sequence of rooms he almost shares the terror of Ferdinand II's little son, the Count of Bari, who at the age of seven was lost for over an hour in the labyrinthine halls.

The decoration of the apartments belongs for the most part to the early and mid-nineteenth century, but a series of rooms still exists which is predominantly eighteenth century in character. The walls are hung with elegant silks from the famous manufactory at San Leucia, gilded rococo scrolls enclose pretty, light amorous paintings by Fischetti and Dominici and cluster about sparkling mirrors and charming stucco reliefs, while floors of patterned marble repeat the lozenges and arabesques of cornice and vault and reflect the gleam of fountain-like chandeliers. Mechanical birds sit in golden cages, one of them ready to burst into trills every time the clock beneath his perch strikes the hour. The theatre, with its gargantuan chandeliers and columns of green marble brought from the Temple of Serapis at Pozzuoli, belongs to the end of this period. It is furnished with a huge portal at the back of the stage which would often be opened during a performance to include the spectacular landscape of the garden in the play.

Yet another and stranger relic of the eighteenth century is the Christmas crib which almost fills a room beyond the library. It consists of hundreds of naturalistic figures in full colour placed in a minutely detailed landscape of rock, ruin and flying angels. Many sculptors of repute worked on this elaborate assemblage, among them Nicola Ingaldi, Lorenzo Mosca, Francesco Celebrano, Matteo Bottiglieri and Battista Polidoro. Its extreme realism excites little enthusiasm today but it is a perfect example of a traditional Neapolitan art, a direct descendant of the medieval miracle plays.

The nineteenth-century apartments at Caserta have been criticised for their neo-classic heaviness, yet they create an atmosphere of royal splendour seldom encountered outside the realm of fantasy, and their bold, exotic colour is unforgettable. Scintillating surfaces, luminous reflections, harmonies of fiery red, white and purple, of grey, gold, rose-yellow and amethyst, of terracotta and crimson, all combine in a grand ceremonial flourish in the Throne Room decorated in 1845 for Ferdinand II by Angelini, Tommaso Arnaud and Genovesi. A gilded winged figure hovers above the lion-armed throne surmounted by flags, and trophies of arms, yellow marble pilasters soar up to the gold-stuccoed vault and a large, fresh painting by Gennaro Maldarelli of Charles III laying the foundation stone of the palace. The floor repeats the stucco motifs within the gigantic hexagons and circles of its gold and blue-grey marbles.

Pompeian influence is naturally strong at Caserta. Stools and chairs strut across the polished floors on bird and animal legs terminating in eagle, lion and sphinx heads, sportive *amorini*, copied from the last style of Pompeian mural painting, enliven the frieze in Francis II's bedroom; and in one of the bathrooms the sarcophagus-shaped, gold-lined bath is arranged like a fountain in a Pompeian garden. The so-called English garden, the creation of Maria Carolina, wife of Ferdinand I, contains a grotto simulating the atmosphere of a Pompeian ruin.

But the English garden is no more than a minor incident in the park at Caserta, the fascination of which lies in the strait-jacket

A statue in the garden representing Terpsichore

The endless corridors and vast apartments could intimidate a visitor

The Hall of Mars, a nineteenth-century apartment with bas-reliefs by Valerio Monreale

RIGHT: *Columns of red marble from Apulia flank the great vestibule*

OPPOSITE: *The Throne Room decorated in 1845 for Ferdinand II*

The royal bathroom, furnished for Francis II with Carrara marble

The Theatre, decorated in 1796, seen from the royal box. The columns are of green marble from the Temple of Serapis at Pozzuoli

layout already perceived through the vestibule. A glinting channel of water caught between grass verges, two broad paths and thick evergreens leads on and on past cascades, past fountains and sculptured groups to the thunderous two-pronged waterfall which feeds them all. The sensation encouraged by the scale of the palace is nowhere so insistent as in this great garden. Some of the statues, especially those in the tableau of Diana and Actaeon, give the uncanny impression that if only they could be caught unawares they would be seen moving about in the landscape, their cold marble flushed with life. They have no bases but stride freely across the rocks in the haphazard attitudes of people playing the game of statues. A yet stranger and more powerful impact is made by the firmly-rooted terminal statues grouped in a semi-circle to announce the lowest of the fountains. Divinely proportioned, intensely alive, they stand against tall yew hedges with fluttering garments, holding out seasonal fruits, signs of the Zodiac or the paraphernalia of the Muses, their lips parted in disquieting, cynical smiles. Above their white bases their uplifted arms are gauntleted in dark, slaty green moss,

OPPOSITE: *Pompeian influences in the decoration of Francis II's bedroom*

The view towards the palace from the top of the cascade where it gushes out from the Carolina Aqueduct

their cheeks and brows are mottled with lichen. Decadent, utterly irresistable, they are the genii loci of Caserta. We do not know who carved them. Tommaso Solari, Paolo Persico, Andrea Violani, Gaetano Salamoni and Angelo Brunelli all worked on the garden sculpture but no record was kept of their individual labours.

Steps mount up beside the final cascade to where it gushes forth from the Carolina Aqueduct specially constructed under Vanvitelli's supervision to bring the water from Monte Taburno more than twenty miles away. From this point the eye is led along the shining avenue of water, past the glittering statues, back to the brooding bulk of the great house floating on the distant haze, a giant's domain. The path does not go on. We are compelled to descend again to the garden, to the statues and the fountains, to retrace all our countless steps, to be engulfed once again by the palace. This is the climax of the whole grandiose, nightmare scheme.

OLIVE COOK

OPPOSITE

ABOVE: *The water for the cascade was brought to Caserta from more than twenty miles away*
BELOW: *The tableau of Diana and Actaeon at the foot of the cascade*

The Royal Palace
TURIN
The former residence of the kings of Sardinia and of Italy

A fountain by Simone Martinez in the garden, which was originally designed by Le Nôtre

IF IT WERE NOT for the chimerical dome of the Cappella della Santa Sindone rising up so strangely to the left of the Royal Palace, nobody would suspect that this sober front concealed an exuberance of gilded, carved, inlaid, painted and looking-glass decoration surpassing the highest flights of fancy. But that exciting outline, combining the undulations of a pagoda with the zigzag step effects of a Mexican extravagance prepares the mind for the shock of the contrast between the incredibly rich interior and the flat, reticent exterior of the palace, so close in spirit to neo-classicism that it is difficult to believe in its seventeenth-century date.

The palace, residence of the kings of Sardinia and of Italy until 1865, stands in the centre of busy, dingy Turin, separated from the north side of the Piazza Castello by an east and a west wing and by a simple bronze railing and two equestrian statues dating from 1846. The four-storey façade is the work of Amedeo, son of Carlo di Castellamonte who had been responsible for the modernisation of the city and had designed the first coherent street in all Italy, the via Roma. Vittorio Amedeo I had decided to build a new palace as early as 1633 but little progress was made until 1646 when the Regent, Maria Cristina, entrusted the design to Castellamonte. By 1663 the long main block of the front and much of the east wing, now the Armoury, were finished. Work continued throughout the reigns of Carlo Emmanuele II, Vittorio Amedeo II, Carlo Emmanuele III and Vittorio Amedeo III, and under the enthusiastic Carlo Alberto there was a final spate of re-decorating in the neo-classic style.

Bernhardt Werner's engraving of the façade of the Royal Palace in 1780

An engraving by John Blaer, dated 1682, showing the garden on the ramparts which Le Nôtre constructed for the King's 'security and pleasure'

PROPVGNACVLVM.
CVI VIRIDE NOMEN
Cum Regii Palatii, atque Hortorum Prospectu
Ad securitatem, atq, delicias
Regiorum Sabaudiæ Ducum.

A nineteenth-century equestrian figure at the gate of the palace, behind which rises the cupola of the Cappella Reale, the work of Guarino Guarini in 1666

RIGHT: A design for a new wing of the palace which was never carried out. It was to contain a gallery ornamented by historical paintings, classical statuary and busts of the royal family

MVSÆI.
cum Regiæ Familiæ sculptis. Gestorumque
pictis Imaginibus, Bibliotheca.
Et Statuarum veterum Ornamentis. Vulgo
LA GALLERIA.
Prospectus interior. Et exterior.

The work of the seventeenth century has been adapted in many of the apartments to the manner of later periods, but there are some vivid survivals. These include in particular numerous ceiling paintings by Daniele Seiter, who arrived in Turin in 1688 and remained there until his death in 1705. The long dining-room, called after the painter the Galleria del Daniele, is dominated by his frescoes of allegorical and mythical subjects. Seiter's style owes something to Pietro da Cortona; it exhibits the same elegance and sophistication and the same breath-taking facility in combining the painted part of the decoration with the bold, gilded stucco of the curving and criss-crossing coffers to create a single grandiose effect. But this first stage in the history of the palace is represented above all by the work of one of the most original of all architects, Guarino Guarini, called to Turin in 1666 by Carlo Emmanuele II. I have already referred to the extraordinary impression made by the exterior of the Cappella della Santa Sindone: the interior is no less remarkable. The House of Savoy possessed one of the holiest of relics, the shroud in which the body of Christ was believed to have been wrapped after his descent from the Cross. Emmanuele Filiberto had brought it from Chambéry to the new capital with the intention of building a church for it, but Carlo Emmanuele decided to erect a large chapel at the east end of the cathedral adjoining the palace and with a door opening directly into it from the royal apartments. Castellamonte had begun the chapel some ten years before Guarini's arrival in Turin and the cylindrical structure had risen as far as the entablature of the lower tier. Upon this Guarini set his fantastic dome. His design makes insistent play with triangular shapes and with multiples of three, thus displaying a compelling symbolism. Three circular vestibules intrude into Castellamonte's original plan, three massive arches span the six bays of the cylinder and then, above a sequence of six windows, wide shallow arches weave in and out, in patterns of threes, ever diminishing in size and leading the eye up and up to a twelve-pointed star, in the centre of which there hovers the Holy Dove lit by twelve oval windows. All the lower part of this chapel is of black marble while the dome is of grey stone, a variation in colour which cleverly enhances the illusion of great distance.

In the following century another man of outstanding genius was closely associated with the palace, Filippo Juvara, who was appointed 'First Architect to the King' in 1714. He himself designed not only the airy Scissor Staircase, named after a motif adorning the second landing, but planned down to the last detail the delicious Chinese Room. It is a square chamber, the walls of which are animated by delicate scrollwork carved to Juvara's designs by Angelo Sariga and a certain Vietto, painted red and gold and enclosing either oval and rectangular panels of

The cupola of the Cappella della Santa Sindone

The Throne Room by Pelagio Palagi, c. 1840

The staircase, built by Augusto Ferri in 1864

The crucifix from the king's private chapel, with inlay work by Pietro Piffetti

black and gold lacquer or silvery mirrors. The coved ceiling above the vigorous undulations of the red-gold cornice is filled with a single painting, *The Judgement of Paris*, a charming rococo work by one of Juvara's protégés, Claudio Beaumont.

Beaumont was also the author of the painted figures floating above the mirror walls of Queen Maria Theresa's room, their graceful limbs mingling in the cloudy recesses of the glass with the discordant images of modern sightseers. But the eye is soon distracted from these by the glittering inlay work of ivory, precious metals and rare woods which covers every piece of furniture and, like a film of hoar frost, emphasises the curves of broken pediments and slender cabriole legs. The effect is magical and is largely the work of Pietro Piffetti, another artist appointed by Juvara. An infinitely skilled craftsman, he was obsessed with the idea of inlaying wood with costly materials, and when he gave free reign to this idiosyncrasy, his art could result in a display of mere virtuosity. The king's minute private chapel provides an example of this. It is characteristic of Piffetti that the tiny chamber should take the form of an oratory masquerading as a miniature library. The altar resembles a writing table and is flanked by tiers of curving shelves. All the woodwork, including the floor, is profusely decorated with inlay work of ivory, mother-of-pearl and various coloured woods. Scrolls, arabesques, swags and cloud shapes mingle with naturalistic clusters of morning glory, roses and peonies and with angels, saints and *putti* bearing emblems of the Passion. It is only the microscopic scale and delicate proportions of the work that redeem this excessive ornament from the charge of vulgarity.

The Mirror Room. Nogari painted the larger portraits directly on the glass

Looking through to the Ballroom, by Palagi, c. 1840

When Juvara died in 1736 he was succeeded by Count Bene-detto Alfieri, the most notable of a series of Piedmontese aristocratic architects. His masterpiece at the Royal Palace is the Mirror Room, where the combination of gilt and reflections is even more bewitching than in Maria Theresa's chamber. It is a small apartment, with walls and ceiling of looking-glass panels framed in gilded scrolls, while the inlaid floor is polished to such a pitch that it too serves as a mirror. It is as though a crystal drop from one of the royal chandeliers had been magnified into a liquid, dazzling room. Swimming across the luminous surfaces are a number of miniatures of members of the Royal House augmented by eleven larger heads of boys, girls and old men painted on the glass by the Venetian Guiseppe Nogari, who also painted the brilliant picture in the centre of the ceiling glass of *Divine Wisdom distributing Sceptres and Crowns*.

Although they do not sparkle with the elegance of the rooms just described, for sheer magnificence and the sumptuous display of royal purple and gold the nineteenth-century decorations at Turin have no equal. The artist in charge of the work under Carlo Alberto was Pelagio Palagi, a Bolognese painter who had studied in Rome. He was working at the palace almost without interruption from 1834 until 1853. Among the first of the apartments to be reconstituted according to Palagi's designs was the Throne Room. He retained the seventeenth-century ceiling, accommodating his own decoration very successfully to the robust pattern of gilded coffers, bold masks and rosettes swirling about an oval allegory by Giovanni Miel set in a rich rectangular frame. Palagi echoed and intensified its warm colouring in his

Within the palace, a wealth of gilded detail

A marble caryatid by Gaggini from the chimneypiece in the Council Chamber

St Agatha, a detail of the engraved ivory inlay work by Piffetti in the king's private chapel, c. 1731

OPPOSITE: *A stool by Pelagio Palagi in the Council Chamber*

treatment of the rest of the room. It is small by comparison with the great throne rooms of some other palaces, but it makes an impression of overwhelming splendour. The lion throne is set on a red velvet-covered dais enclosed by a gilt bronze railing, the coils of which are composed of curling fern fronds, garlands, full quivers, flaming torches, doves, putti and urns. And above the throne purple curtains fringed with gold and silver lustre billow from a gilded circular canopy.

From the Throne Room a whole suite of apartments opens out, all decorated by Palagi and varying in colour from scarlet and gold to grass green and gold. Among the rich furnishings there are some stools designed by Palagi which merit particular attention. They are fashioned of gilt bronze and the supports take the form of winged youths flying out from under the seat to hold hands or clasp a wreath. The green and gold Council Chamber boasts four superb standing gilded candelabra, each branching out into figures and foliage above four crowned classical maidenly forms resting on a dolphin base. Female caryatids flank the white marble mantelpiece and their counterparts in gilded bronze frame the mirror above it. They were carved by two forgotten artists, F. Somani and Giuseppe Gagani. The seventeenth-century ceiling of this noble room shows female heads, large and powerfully modelled, half turned away from the spectator, the full throats ending in massy foliage.

But the climax of Palagi's transformations at Turin is the amazing Alcove Room, once the bedroom of Carlo Emmanuele II, now a spirited, fairground riot of gleaming gilt. The ordering of the apartment, divided in two by an elaborate screen, is basically seventeenth-century with a splendid ceiling decorated with trophies of arms and winged figures; but to the nineteenth century belong the gilded half-length female forms swelling from tapering columns to support the entablature of the screen.

Palagi seems to have been most inspired when confronted with existing decorations. The great pilastered Ballroom, only completed in Carlo Alberto's reign, is all Palagi's invention, and although it abounds in charming detail, the apartment makes an impression of coldness and formality. By the time it was finished the palace seemed to be complete in every detail. But in 1864 Vittorio Emmanuele II commissioned Augusto Ferri to build the marble staircase which now leads stiffly and pompously from the state rooms down to the inner courtyard. It is a startlingly white and raw sienna composition adorned with life-size statues of the princes of Savoy and large Edwardian-looking urns. A colossal equestrian figure charging from a shell niche urges the visitor from the foot of the stairs to the courtyard entrance, and he is finally shown through the door by a crisply carved Prince Eugene.

OLIVE COOK

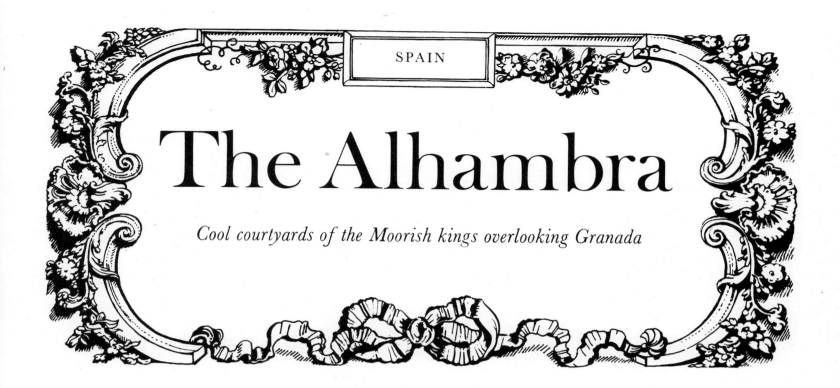

The Alhambra

Cool courtyards of the Moorish kings overlooking Granada

IT IS THE IMAGINATIVE SETTING of the Alhambra which stars the originality of the Arabs and not only demonstrates them as being decorators of genius but, above all, eminent poets in the siting of their fortresses. Seen from the heights above Albaicin, the rectangular geometry of the twenty or more towers shows a magnificent Cézanne-like rhythm of descent down to the ravine below. Though sharp black stabs of tall cypress trees give some hint of the many hidden courtyards, yet for all its intricacies the Alhambra remains secret and even austere, as compared with any trellised and domed rose-pink Moghul palace. Together with the gardens of the Generalife, the setting of this unique citadel is further enhanced by a magnificent backdrop – the perpetual white-capped brilliance of the Sierra Nevada, shimmering against the cloudless turquoise sky.

Sheltered within these massive fortified walls, by a sheer miracle, survives a series of most delicate and fragile of structures – part palace and harem, part residence for court officials and their entourages. The gradual additions over two decades encompass the changes and expansions necessary for the way of life in a newly founded outpost of a great empire. Designed by the descendants of nomads, living a tented existence in the desert, accustomed to upheavals attendant on conquests dictated by political gain and religious fervour, they still retain some aspects of provisional and temporary buildings.

Yet of the actual designers of the Alhambra, there is no certain record. Said to have been built by Christian slave labour, their Arab supervisors and designers were the masters of space,

The Moorish palace of the Alhambra rises upon its crag ('El Ultimo Suspiro del Moro') dominating the roof-tops of Granada

OPPOSITE: *The building of the Court of the Lions was begun in 1377 by Mohammed V. It is surrounded by 124 slender alabaster columns*

An engraving from Swinburn's Travels in Spain, 1775 *and* 1776, *showing the situation of the Alhambra with the cathedral and the city of Granada on the right and the Generalife at the top left of the picture. The two main towers were known as the Torre de Comares (centre) and the Torre de la Campana (right)*

scale and decoration, for these towers, halls and audience chambers open onto cool slender-columned courtyards of serene proportions, which have as a basis the simplest architectural elements, all within the classical traditions of Greece and Rome. Filled with the sound of birds, murmuring fountains and soft intonations of the Koran – the echo of whose very words seem forever held and endlessly repeated in the Cufic script which enriches the walls – they were originally bright with colour. Today, apart from panels of polychrome ceramic, scarcely a trace of this painted decoration remains. The effect was not so overpowering as at first may be supposed, for this juxtaposition of turquoise, scarlet, violet, gold and green, minutely disposed throughout the intricately carved plaster spandrils, had an iridescent quality reminiscent of the great temple of Kumbakonam, where tier upon tier of life-size images, prismatic and crude in colour, which, on the principle of a pointilliste painting, appear from a distance in the brilliant light of southern India as a vast shimmering blue-white obelisk.

A nineteenth-century view of the Alhambra. The lower building on the right is the palace of Charles V which was never completed. It was designed by Pedro Machuca, who had studied under Michelangelo

The Arabs who designed these delicately arcaded patios, with their theatrical enfilades, were equally masters of lighting. Full use was made of the sunlight flooding the courtyards and reflected upwards from the dazzling marble floors and pools into the adjacent loggias, to catch the undersides of elaborate plasterwork panels, subtly gilded and outlined with vermilion shadows, forming grilles of golden filigree under the shady arcades.

Higher up, too, the honeycombed cupolas appear to have been largely decorated with cool blue and white, cross-lighted by intricately pierced *jalousies*, starred with multi-coloured glass which, with the early morning and evening sun, made kaleidoscopic patterns of magical and ethereal lightness. By night this effect was duplicated in a more mysterious way, by dimly diffused light from great swaying glass lanterns, suspended from hooks still to be seen in the centres of each cupola.

Not only in the courtyards, but inside the buildings also, the important element of water has been introduced. The cooling sounds and magic image of those narrow glinting streams which

The Court of the Lions, a Moorish masterpiece

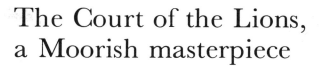

A detail of the upper part of an archway

The fountain is supported by twelve beasts

LEFT: *The stalactite ornamentation of the ceilings produces an astonishingly rich effect*

ABOVE LEFT: *Charles V's fountain underneath the walls*

ABOVE RIGHT: *Massive towers surround the palace*

run from pools and fountains through shaded halls and pavilions, not only have a practical value but serve to recall that, for the Arab mind, purification by water has a profound religious significance, and however luxurious and colourful palace life may have been here in the past, it was forever tempered by the all-pervading religious austerities of Islam.

Even now, in the smoky blue light of a spring dusk, the sound of the nerve-tearing east wind, wearing away the very fibres of the plaster-work, seems to echo those cries which used to greet the first-seen slim, slow-rising crescent of the new moon, long anticipated from every mirador and tower by eager watchers, happy to end the month-long tensions of Ramadan. From below would follow the soft tread of hennaed feet, swiftly running toward the great vaulted bakehouses where soon arises the scent of charcoal fires and meat roasts. The palace springs to life with the lighting of a thousand lamps placed in every niche, and row upon row of waiting slippers quickly donned as countless servants arrange heavy woven carpets, billowing cushions and low charcoal braziers, to form groups for the many waiting officials below the great dais where reclines the Caliph and his court. More lustrous silk-piled carpets suspended from long metal rods across every archway and banquet hall, enclose the noisy diners and screen them from the prying eyes of the women in the galleries above. Then, across the courtyards a procession of bearers carrying pyramids of sugar-dusted sweets, pomegranate seeds in shallow silver trays, tall sprinklers of rose-water and the many little cakes prepared on slabs of marble over stone troughs, packed with fresh snow brought in great thonged earthen jars by patient stumbling donkeys from the Sierra Nevada.

Today, stripped bare and despoiled, scarcely any furnishings remain to remind us of this well organised palace life.

Until the day when the Cross of the Reconquest was planted on the Torre de la Vela, much of the history of its development is uncertain. The summit of the Asabica, the Moorish name for the hill on which the Alhambra stands, was certainly fortified from ancient times and grew in importance in the ninth century, when this region was dominated by the Emirs of nearby Cordoba. Formerly it faced a similar fortification on the opposite hill of Albaicin – the palace of the Berber chieftain Zagui ben Ziri, a descendant of the Royal Family of Tunis. In 1238 Mohammed ben Alhamar, vassal of the Christian King San Fernando, occupied Granada, having first seized the fortified citadels of Jaen, Baeza and Guadix. With great vision, it was he who then devised the system, a series of reservoirs, whereby the water from the river Darro was raised to the top of the hill, and which enabled him to transform the citadel into a mighty *Alhisan* or fortress, within whose protecting walls he started to build palaces and gardens, known as Al Qala al-Hambra – 'The Red Fortress' – later to become La Alhambra – of today.

In the days of Mohammed ben Alhamar the top of the Asabica was divided into two parts by a ravine which contained the reservoirs (court of the Cisterns). The main watchtower and keep (Alcayaba) was constructed on the west promontory over foundations which had remained from ancient times, and being of massive construction have survived in their original thirteenth-century style with but few modifications. On the opposite side, he built his palace (La Alhambra) and the Residence (Alhambra Alta) which housed his officials and harem.

The inspired patronage of the succession of monarchs who enlarged and elaborated the Alhambra is commemorated and praised in the incised plasterwork, the decoration of which reaches a climax of technical brilliance in what is happily the best preserved and most complete part of the old palace: the Hall of the Two Sisters.

Above friezes inscribed with verses, by Ibn Xamrak, in honour of a son of Mohammed V, the great cupola is composed entirely of *mocarobes* (stalactite vaults) and rests on an octagonal base. The four pseudo-pendentives which effect the transition of the square to the octagon are also of *mocarobes* – the resulting

Bas-relief at the entrance to Charles V's palace

The elaborate architrave and medallion above one of the side doors to Charles V's palace

147

geometric complexity of design, as in the similar cupola of the Hall of the Abercerrajes on the other side of the Court of Lions, is of exceptional grace and lightness, and seems to float over the apartment.

It is above the Hall of Abercerrajes that there exists a miniature house, complete with its own patio, undoubtedly the apartment of some favourite during the times when much of the court life was centred on this part of the old palace. More than probably it was in the Great Hall below, that Mulez Abul Hassan ordered the decapitation of all his sons by his former wife, so that the throne might pass to Boabdil, the child of his second love, Zoraya.

It later fell to the lot of this Boabdil to organise the removal of the remains of all his ancestors from the royal mausoleum in order to take them to a safer resting place in Mondujar – an ignoble end for this great line of twenty-five ruling monarchs.

The final capitulation to the Catholic Kings followed in 1492, that same tumultous year which saw the discovery of America. In the days of magnificence which followed, the Emperor Charles V, while on his wedding journey, stayed at the Alhambra: captivated by the site, he was inspired to build one of the most splendid renaissance palaces outside of Italy.

For this new royal residence he had as architect Pedro Machuca, a veritable eagle of the Spanish renaissance, who had studied under no less a master than Michelangelo himself. Built alongside the fragile Moorish palace each serves to complement the other by means of contrast.

It is fortunate that many of these splendid buildings are still intact in spite of the many subsequent untoward happenings: an explosion in 1590, the many changes made to suit the altered domestic requirements of the Court of the Catholic Kings, havoc wrought by Napoleonic troops, romantic additions and restorations made during the nineteenth century, earthquakes, and lastly a disastrous fire in 1890. More recently, in the Court of the Lions, the cupola of the eastern pavilion has been replaced by a tiled roof, which, though reminiscent of that shown in David Robert's drawing, is unhappily of overpowering height and heaviness. The fountain, however, has been restored to its original appearance by the removal of the second bowl, which was presumably added early in the nineteenth century, when extensive changes were made to the gardens. The admirable gardens of Lindaraja and Generalife, we are told, are of recent date, but such beauty may be nearer to the originals than is generally supposed, for the elements of garden design do not change throughout the ages. Formal gardens seldom mature in a single life-span and their charm and mystery is often fleeting, and to maintain perfection must constantly be replanted.

ANTHONY DENNEY

The circular courtyard in the palace of Charles V

A waterspout, dating from the sixteenth century

OPPOSITE: *The Court of the Lions which, in Moorish days, was planted with trees and flowers*

Aranjuez

Philip II's leafy palace on the banks of the River Tagus

ARANJUEZ, AT THE confluence of the Tagus and Jarama rivers, about thirty miles south of Madrid, is the most celebrated of the rare oases which break the arid monotony of most of Spain. The air resounds with the noise of rushing water, the trees are the finest in southern Europe and the nightingales (which were Philip II's chief regret during three years' absence in Portugal) are as renowned as the strawberries and asparagus from its market-gardens.

In the Middle Ages the land belonged to the knights of Santiago, whose Grand Master, Lorenzo Suarez de Figueroa, erected a castle there in 1387. When Ferdinand and Isabella merged the Grand Mastership in the Crown, the property passed with it. Charles V converted the building into a hunting-lodge, which Juan Bautista de Toledo and Juan de Herrera, the architects of the Escorial, replaced by a palace for Philip II. This was twice damaged by fire and restored under Philip V by his Overseer of Works, Pedro Caro Idrogo, following Herrera's plans. A third fire broke out in 1748 and the present exterior of the building dates from the reign of Ferdinand VI and is the work of Santiago Bonavia. This native of Piacenza, one of the many foreign artists introduced to Spain by Philip V's Queen, Elisabeth Farnese, has given the complex of earlier periods a unified Italian rococo character. His style was faithfully reproduced by Francesco Sabatini, Vanvitelli's son-in-law, in the two wings erected between 1772 and 1778 on the west side to enclose the great paved and cobbled entrance court. In shape a square round a central courtyard, two storeys high, the building is of a

The entrance to the Garden of the Prince which was laid out by Charles IV, as Prince of the Asturias

OPPOSITE: *The mock-Moorish smoking-room was added to the palace at Aranjuez by Alfonso XII who took the idea from the Alhambra*

The Royal Palace at Aranjuez drawn by an army officer, Domingo de Aguirre, in 1773

Philip II's elms still shade the avenues of Aranjuez, of which the largest is called the 'Salon de los Reyes Católicos'

lively pink brick, broken by stone pilasters, arcading and bold curved or pointed pediments. The upper windows have balconies, the lower ones are screened by heavy grilles. Over a *porte cochère* of five arches, the centre of the façade rises to three storeys with an elaborate pediment on which stand statues of Philip II, Philip V and Ferdinand VI. Two shallow domes at each end of the façade, suggesting the influence of Filippo Juvara, the great Piedmontese architect who ended his career in Spain, originally covered the chapel and theatre.

The inside of the palace has none of the unity which Bonavia succeeded in giving to the exterior, though the fine main staircase, with busts by Coysevox of Louis XIV, Marie Thérèse of Austria and the Grand Dauphin, is his. Until late in the eighteenth century it was furnished only when the court was in residence; the pictures, collected indiscriminately by Charles IV, included, Beckford noticed, 'innumerable trash'. Many of the rooms were tawdrily decorated for Isabel II, and Alfonso XII added a mock-Moorish smoking-room imitated from the Alhambra at Granada. The palace contains, however, one of the most extraordinary rococo décors in Europe, the porcelain room in the north-east corner. Apart from four inset mirrors, the whole surface of the walls and ceiling is lined with porcelain plaques, the lower panels decorated with *singeries*, the upper with large groups of Chinese figures in bold relief. At first sight the profusion of incident and vivid colouring are almost unbearably

The west side of the palace; the domes at each end originally covered the chapel and theatre

dazzling. The porcelain comes from the Buen Retiro factory which Charles III established with workmen brought from Capodimonte, and the room, completed about 1765, bears the signature of their director, Giuseppe Gricci.

The large dining-room, designed by Bonavia, has a series of paintings by the Neapolitan, Corrado Giaquinto, a ceiling frescoed by the Venetian, Jacopo Amigoni, and a *scagliola* floor inlaid with musical and military trophies. Here tourists like Joseph Townsend, Rector of Pewsey (the Tagus valley at Aranjuez reminded him of the Vale of Pewsey), were admitted to watch the Royal Family at dinner. On the north side is a small vaulted chapel, frescoed by Francisco Bayeu, Goya's brother-in-law. Ferdinand VI, the patron of Scarlatti, added a theatre, with a ceiling by Raphael Mengs, where Italian opera was regularly performed. This was dismantled shortly before Beckford's visit in 1794. 'Not later than last summer', he wrote, 'this grand theatrical apartment was divided into a suite of shabby, band-boxical rooms for the accommodation of the Infant of Parma. No mercy was shown to the beautiful roof. In some places, legs and folds of drapery are still visible; but the workmen are hammering and plastering at a great rate, and in a few days whitewash will cover all'. This, incidentally, was not the first time that music was heard in Aranjuez; Philip V was invariably accompanied by the great *castrato* Farinelli, who was under contract to sing the same four arias every day of the year as the only

The fountain of Hercules in the Garden of the Island, erected in 1661 by Philip IV

A detail of the façade, rebuilt in 1752

A vaulted arcade on the courtyard level, with a flagged and cobbled floor

means of relieving the King's acute attacks of melancholia.

Aranjuez's beautiful gardens have long been famous. The oldest is the Garden of the Island in a loop of the Tagus on the north side of the palace; a narrow canal, the Ría, has been cut across the base. Philip II introduced elms here from England, and in spring it is a paradise of shade and running water. As Saint Simon remarked in 1722: 'There are all sorts of curiosities in the shape of artificial trees with birds perched in them, which let fall showers of water when one walks underneath; water also squirts from the statues and from the mouths of animals, so that an unwary visitor finds himself drenched without possibility of escape. To any one accustomed to the beautiful gardens laid out by Le Nôtre, all this seems trivial and in bad taste; nevertheless, in Castille these gardens appear charming; they are so green and shady, and so well watered.' The garden's original formality has been softened by time, and its most striking feature is now a splendid avenue of plane trees parallel with the Tagus. Seven fountains with classical statues, erected by Philip III and IV, are still to be seen, but the pergolas, arbours, alcoves and grottoes illustrated by Juan Alvárez de Colmenar in *Les Délices de l'Espagne* have all disappeared.

The much smaller parterre garden on the east side of the palace was laid out by Etienne Boutelou, a French expert summoned by Philip V to create the gardens at La Granja. Magnolias, laburnum and ilexes break the regularity of the design, which includes four pools originally containing groups of sculpture by another Frenchman, Antoine Dumandré. Two of his nymphs caressing dragons are left, but the others have been replaced by a neo-classic Ceres and an elaborate Hercules and Antaeus. A neat box *parterre* at the south-east corner of the palace, known as the Garden of Philip II, is lined with brick niches which once held marble busts of Roman emperors.

Beyond the suspension bridge that has succeeded an earlier structure, whose four terminal statues of the Continents remain, stretches the large Garden of the Prince, laid out by Charles IV as Prince of the Asturias. It has every fashionable embellishment of the time, a Chinese garden with banana-plants, an English garden presented by Charles III's Irish Minister, Richard Wall, classical pavilions and fountains dedicated to Apollo and Narcissus. Plane avenues lead to the enchanting Casa del Labrador, the Spanish Petit Trianon, where Charles IV would go to amuse himself by cooking lamb's fry and garlic omelettes.

The forest and pastures beyond the Tagus have at different times been populated by teams of camels employed in hauling timber and by a model Friesian dairy herd. Their plentiful game provided Charles III, who became ill if he could not shoot every day, with his chief enjoyment. While at Aranjuez he used to wear the black shooting-breeches in which he was portrayed

by Goya even for his morning audiences in order to lose no time changing. The woods are crossed by long vistas, though to the west these have been sadly obstructed by farm buildings.

The chief square of the small town is the Plaza de San Antonio, built by Bonavia in the same stone and pink brick as the palace, and terminated by the charming round Church of St Anthony, with a shallow dome and eccentrically large lantern. When the King was in residence, the town bustled with activity and travellers found living exorbitantly dear; Joseph Townsend had to pay eight shillings and fourpence for 'one miserable bedroom'. But the diplomats and courtiers were not much better off; for most of the century they were lodged in hovels half underground, until Charles III was persuaded to build better quarters when a carriage fell through the roof of the Papal Nuncio's dining-room. Aranjuez enjoyed a raffish Indian summer under Ferdinand VII, who filled the palace with lovely Señoras and Andalusian bull-fighters. Five years after his death George Borrow already noticed the forlorn air that strikes us today: 'Intriguing courtiers no longer crowd its halls; its spacious circus, where Manchegan bulls once roared in rage and agony, is now closed, and the light tinkling of guitars is no longer heard amidst its groves and gardens.'

ANTHONY HOBSON

The Ballroom in the Casita del Labrador, close by the main palace. This little palace was built by Charles IV at the end of the eighteenth century, and the interior is decorated in the 'Pompeian' style

Philip II had a strong preference for the most austere architectural style

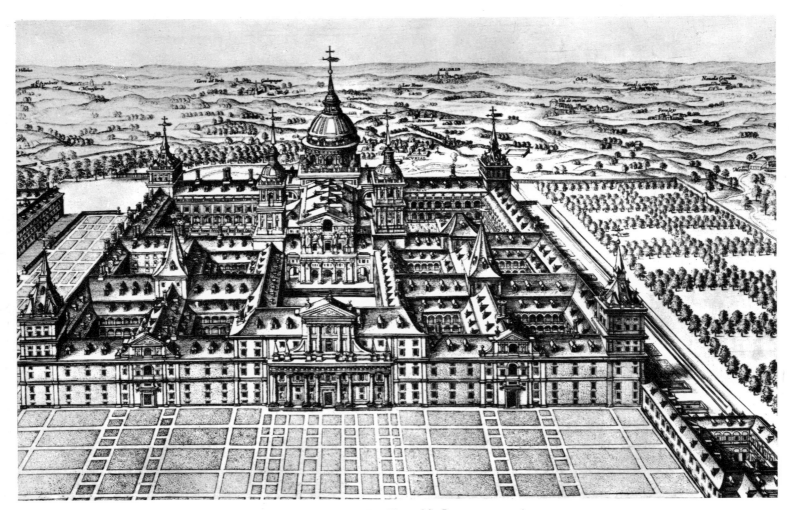

The palace contains ten courtyards grouped round the huge central Basilica of St Lawrence

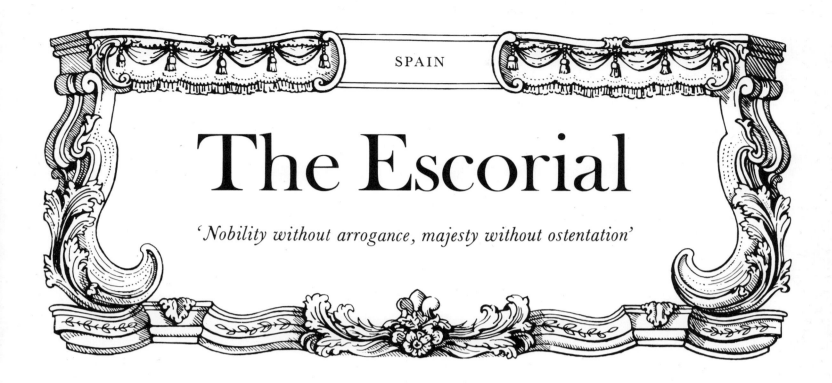

The Escorial

'Nobility without arrogance, majesty without ostentation'

THE FIRST SIGHT OF the Escorial is breath-taking, whether seen from the mountains against the rocky outcrops and stunted willows of the plain, or from a rise in the Madrid road, reddish-brown against the bleak Guadarramas. A distant view-point is needed to appreciate its merits of mass and proportion, as well as the subtle variety of the roof-line: the dome and two bell-towers of the church at the centre, the slender spires of the towers at each corner and the pedimented elevation above two rows of engaged columns over the principal door. Approaching closer, these qualities tend to be forgotten in face of the oppressive monotony of the walls, on which the plain windows scarcely project, renouncing even the ornament of light and shade.

The Royal Monastery of St Lawrence (to give the correct title) is a huge quadrilateral, 225 yards long (half the length of Versailles) by 175 yards wide, enclosing a basilica. Its suggestion of the Kremlin, even of the Potala, is not unfounded, for it was conceived as a fortress of Catholic art, science and religion against the Northern heretics. It contains a school in the north-west corner, whose most notable pupil, ironically enough, was Manuel Azaña, the Republican President whose anti-clerical convictions, in violent reaction from his school-days, were among the origins of the Civil War. The monastery occupies the south side of the building, with the cloisters, known as the Patio of the Evangelists, adjoining the church. Their chief feature is an elegant domed pavilion at the centre of four water-tanks, with statues of the Evangelists at the corners.

Between school and monastery is the Courtyard of the Kings,

The Courtyard of the Kings

Two of six statues on the façade of the basilica

entered from the principal door. This faces the pedimented façade of the basilica, decorated with six gigantic statues of Old Testament monarchs by J. B. Monegro, with gilt crowns and sceptres, on an architrave supported by massive Doric columns. The basilica is of impressive size and the same bare granite as the rest of the building. In the shape of a Greek cross, its lofty dome is carried by four huge piers faced with fluted pilasters. Apart from some later ceiling frescoes by Luca Giordano, the decoration is concentrated round the high altar. This stands in front of a *retablo* of four tiers of jasper columns with gilt capitals and bases, the spaces between filled with paintings or gilt statues. In an arched recess on either side, at the centre of a screen of Doric columns of the same material, kneels a group of gilt figures by the Milanese Leone and Pompeo Leoni: on the left Charles V attended by his wife, daughter and two sisters; opposite, Philip II with three of his four wives (Mary I of England is absent) and his eldest son, Don Carlos, the hero of Verdi's opera.

On the north and west the Escorial is surrounded by a wide terrace, on the two sides facing the plain by a formal garden of box *parterres* alternating with flights of stairs leading down to grottoes, now empty and decayed. At the south-west angle is the charming arcaded infirmary, the most elegant piece of architecture in the whole complex. Below the terrace, ducks and

Chinese geese have taken over the square fishpond against a majestic background of balustrade and blind arcading.

It was on St Lawrence's day, August 10, 1557, that Philip II received the news of the victory at St Quentin and vowed to build a monastery dedicated to the great Spanish martyr, to be served by monks of the Hieronymite Order in whose convent at Yuste his father, the Emperor Charles V, had died. A two years' survey for a site was made after his return to Spain. Practical reasons were given for the final choice of a spur of the Guadarramas: nearness to Madrid, cool summer climate, abundance of water and of granite for building; but the wild grandeur of the landscape, so much in harmony with his aesthetic conception, must have been a decisive factor. Work on the foundations started in 1562. The ground-plan was drawn by Juan Bautista de Toledo, who had worked under Michelangelo on St Peter's; he died in 1567 and was succeeded by Juan de Herrera, who had studied in Flanders and Italy and was a disciple of Vignola. But Philip II supervised his architects in every detail and frequently changed their plans. The *estilo desornamentado* – basically classicism of the high renaissance stripped of the 'vanity' of unnecessary ornament – of which the Escorial is the outstanding example, was his own individual creation. 'Simplicity in the

ABOVE: *Titian's portrait of the Hapsburg Emperor Charles V, who was also King of Spain*

ABOVE LEFT: *Philip II of Spain, a portrait by Alonso Sanchez Coello*

OPPOSITE

ABOVE: *The study and bedroom of Philip II. The bed is that in which he died. On the walls of the study hang pictures by Dürer and Bosch*
BELOW: *Another room in King Philip II's private apartments, with relics of his occupation, including his astrolabe. All the walls in this suite of rooms were half-tiled*

The Basilica of St Lawrence is an imitation on a smaller scale of the plan of St Peter's, Rome

A room in the Casita del Principe built for the Infante Don Carlos in 1772 by Charles III, and decorated in the fashionable Pompeian style

It was monastery, museum and royal residence combined

The Library at the Escorial is among the most splendid libraries in the world. In the bookcases, designed by Juan de Herrera, the volumes are arranged in the renaissance manner with the gilt fore-edges outwards. It contains 45,000 printed books and 5,000 codices

The Hall of Battles was decorated for Philip II by N. Granella and Fabricio Castello with scenes of Spanish victories, including the Battle of Lepanto and the Battle of Higueruela in 1431

The Sala Capitular, which was used by King Philip as a museum for works of art, including El Greco's painting of St Maurice 'in his bad second style', which Philip rejected for the church

163

Details of two tapestries at the Escorial, made by Gobelin after designs by Goya. Above is The Man with a Cloak *and above right is* The Card-players, *woven in about 1778. They hang in the suite of rooms furnished by the Bourbon kings. Most of Goya's original designs for the tapestries are in the Prado, Madrid*

construction, severity in the whole, nobility without arrogance, majesty without ostentation' were the criteria he laid down for Herrera. Philip urged the work on energetically; even so, the construction was not completed till 1584.

Religious observances and the arts were Philip II's two hobbies and much of the last fourteen years of his life was spent in decorating the Escorial. His choice of artists – Italian Mannerists of mediocre talent – was not fortunate, though the frescoes of Castilian victories over the Moors in the Hall of Battles, although drastically restored, have much interest and charm. Little now survives of his collections of drawings, maps, architectural designs and natural history specimens, and the parks, pavilions and herds of deer with which he surrounded the palace, have all disappeared. Even his collection of relics has suffered depredation and its chief treasure, a feather from the wing of the Archangel Gabriel which Beckford saw, 'full three feet long, and of a blushing hue more soft and delicate than that of the loveliest rose', is no longer mentioned. But Benvenuto Cellini's crucifix, a present from the Grand-Duke of Tuscany, is in the upper choir, and there are some magnificent pictures: two Bosches and a Patinir in the palace, Roger van der Weyden's *Crucifixion* and El Greco's *Dream of Philip II* and *Martyrdom of St Maurice* (commissioned for a side-chapel of the Basilica but rejected by the King) in the Sala Capitular. The library contains one of the finest collections of manuscripts in the world, among them the Greek codices collected in Venice by Philip's ambassador, Diego Hurtado de Mendoza, and bound in his heraldic tinctures, one cover red, the other green. It is a superb vaulted room over the main entrance, the ceiling frescoed by Pellegrino Tibaldi and his Spanish assistant, Bartolomé Carducho. In the bookcases, designed by Juan de Herrera, the volumes are arranged in the renaissance manner with the gilt fore-edges outwards.

The palace projects from the east end of the building to form the handle of the gridiron (the instrument of St Lawrence's martyrdom) which is said to have inspired the ground-plan. Apart from the Throne Room and Hall of the Ambassadors, its rooms are small and agreeably unpretentious, with superb views. The floors are of brick, the walls originally hung with Cordova leather above a dado of blue tiles. Here Philip spent each summer, using the time which could be spared from the detailed administration of his empire to join in the church services and conduct visitors in person round the building. Special occasions enlivened the routine, the arrival of a whale's jawbone for the natural history collection, a bullfight given by Don Juan of Austria, sacred dances by seminarists to celebrate Corpus Christi, processions of flagellants invoking the Virgin's intercession for the success of the Armada. Here, in 1598, in an alcove overlooking the high altar, Philip II died after an atrocious illness lasting seven weeks. For a century after his death his rooms were sealed, until Philip V entered against the Prior's resistance.

Philip II did not live to build the royal mausoleum which was part of his original plan, though he had conveyed to the Escorial, in solemn procession through the kingdom, the bodies of his father, mother, grandmother and two aunts. The *Panteon de los Reyes*, under the high altar, was commenced in 1617 after a design by the Roman painter G. B. Crescenzi, and not completed till 1654. An elegant baroque affair of jasper, porphyry and black marble with ormolu enrichments, it is the most frivolous interior in the building. Here the bodies of eleven Spanish sovereigns were escorted by day-long cortèges of plumed and draped horses, monks, penitents, courtiers and officers of state, to be interred (after a preliminary period of decomposition in the *Putridero*) in sarcophagi on the left of the altar, facing their consorts on the opposite wall. The place was a favourite resort of the two last Spanish Hapsburgs; Philip IV used to lie in the niche reserved for him while a requiem Mass was celebrated, and his son, Charles II, would come to gaze for hours at the mummified remains of his ancestors.

The Bourbon kings furnished a suite of rooms which now contain a superb series of tapestries after Goya's cartoons, and built the enchanting miniature *Casita del Principe* in a pine-wood below the monastery. Since then the Escorial has suffered many depredations, notably its systematic looting by the French in 1808. A careful restoration is still in progress.

ANTHONY HOBSON

The Sausage-seller, *a tapestry by Bayeu in the Casita del Principe*

El Greco's The Martyrdom of St Maurice

Sintra

The palace of the Portuguese sovereigns in the Moorish style

A courtyard in the centre of the palace. The fountain is composed of three twisted columns surmounted by small sculptured figures of boys. Beyond is the fine Manueline portal leading to the old bathing grotto

OPPOSITE: *The most remarkable feature of the sky-line of the palace is the pair of conical chimneys which rise above the ancient kitchen*

'THE ALHAMBRA ITSELF cannot well be more morisco in point of architecture than this confused pile which crowns the summit of a rocky eminence and is broken into a variety of picturesque recesses and projections.' This description of Sintra Palace, which William Beckford entered in his journal on Sunday, September, 2, 1787, has been echoed again and again by subsequent visitors, who have thereby, consciously or unconsciously, subscribed to the tradition that the building dates from the period of the Saracenic occupation of Portugal.

Many of its features are indeed strikingly Moorish in design, especially the pair of conical chimneys resembling giant Kentish oast-houses – oriental relations to that of Glastonbury, and distant cousins to those that adorn the seraglio of Abdul the Damned at Istanbul. The first glimpse of these sky-scraping dunce's caps, obtrusively visible from all points of the compass, tends to confirm the assumption that the heterogeneous mass of masonry beneath is of Moorish origin. Closer inspection, however, reveals that Sintra Palace is a medley of half a dozen different architectural styles, none of which is earlier than the fourteenth century.

The remains of a former palace, erected here in the eighth century by the Arab conquerors of the Peninsula and subsequently inhabited by the Moorish kings of Lisbon (yet another factor contributing to the myth of the present structure's origin), are known to have still existed in the reign of King Denis (1279–1325), but it was a later monarch, Dom João I (1385–1433), who founded on the site of these ruins the essentially gothic nucleus of the building which stands today. To him are due the four-

ABOVE AND BELOW: *Two early nineteenth-century views of Sintra. In the upper picture the palace is seen from the road to Mafra and in the lower, from the Lisbon road*

Sintra in the seventeenth century, seen from the south

arched porch at the top of the great flight of steps leading up to the entrance, the principal halls, the kitchen and the chapel, and he it was who first used Sintra as a Portuguese royal residence.

It was from here that he projected his successful Moroccan campaign culminating in the capture of Ceuta in 1415 and here, in 1429, that he received the embassy despatched by Philip the Good, Duke of Burgundy, to request the hand of the Portuguese monarch's daughter, Dona Isobel. The gifts which the duke's ambassadors bore for the prospective bride included a pair of white swans, which so delighted the young Infanta that she had crown-shaped collars of gold made for them and her father ordered a tank to be built for them in the central patio, level with the window of one of the great halls, where she could sit and watch them. When, two years later, she left for her new home in Flanders, he had the ceiling of this hall decorated by his painter, Alvaro de Pedro, with twenty-seven hexagonal panels, each depicting a gold-collared swan, in memory of his daughter and her pets.

A neighbouring hall was likewise decorated by Dom João I, but for a very different reason. Here, at an unspecified date, he was surprised by his English wife, Philippa, John of Gaunt's daughter, in the act of kissing one of her ladies-in-waiting; whereupon, with commendable presence of mind, he quoted his own motto *Por bem*, a phrase which may be freely translated *Honi soit qui mal y pense*, and to commemorate the incident he ordered the roof under which it had occurred to be painted with a multitude of magpies (representing, presumably, his chattering courtiers), each one holding this device in its beak.

Yet another ceiling, that of the chapel, is due to João I, who, abiding perhaps by the tradition that this part of the palace was

The Stag Room, built by Dom Manoel to commemorate the achievements of Portuguese heroes

possibly the original Arab mosque, ordered it to be made in a Moorish design, of painted wood. Following his example, a later king, Dom Manoel I (1495–1521), had the floor of the chapel tiled in a pattern to represent the carpet on which the Moors used to prostrate themselves in the direction of Mecca.

The other Moorish elements which Dom Manoel introduced are no doubt derived from the Spanish *mudejar* style with which his progress through Castile in 1497 would have acquainted him, and these, together with the maritime features inspired by the voyages of Vasco da Gama and with the exotic motifs borrowed from the newly discovered lands beyond the Seven Seas, are typical of the architecture – or, to be more precise, the form of architectural adornment – to which this monarch gave his name. It was to the embellishment of essentially gothic structures that the Manueline builders and decorators applied themselves, and to them are due the distinctively Arab pyramid-capped merlons along the parapets of Sintra and the two-light windows (*ajimeces*), built between 1507 and 1520, 'all of an oriental fantastic shape, crinkled and crankled, and supported by twisted pillars of smooth marble,' recalling those of Seville.

Most of the interior of the palace is likewise typically Manueline in its treatment of certain features, notably Moorish carpentry (*alfarge*) and ceramic (*azulejo*) techniques adumbrating future developments. Over sixty different designs of *azulejo* are represented, from the simple green-and-white chequer-board, reminiscent of Persian work, on the walls of the Hall of Swans, to the intricate raised pattern of dark-green vine-leaves and turquoise-blue acanthus in the Patio of Diana, a little courtyard with a fountain bearing a graceful figure of the divine huntress. Similar tiles in a raised vine-leaf pattern, not unlike that of Victorian Wedgwood plates, adorn the walls of the state bedroom, and the door of the antechamber is framed in rare black tiles dating back to the reign of João I. A further example of *azulejo* work is provided by the so-called Moorish Bathroom, a dependency of the central patio, the walls of which are pierced with concealed jets of water – an ingenious device of the original Arab engineers – and decorated with eighteenth-century blue-and-white picture tiles which show an astonishing development in technique from the early geometric designs, such as the blue-and-green zig-zag pattern in the oldest part of the building now known as the Moorish Dining-room.

Dom João I's taste for painted ceilings was evidently inherited by his successors, for most of the rooms which were constructed long after his death are similarly decorated, notably the antechamber of the state bedroom, in which a ship is depicted surrounded by mermaids rising up from the sea, and a vast hall occupying the whole of the square tower, built in 1508, which is a prominent feature of the exterior of the palace. Here the

The ceiling of the Stag Room, which is divided into seventy-two panels, each containing a stag with the arms of one of the principal noble families

OPPOSITE: *The ceiling of the Hall of Swans was painted for Dom João I in memory of his daughter, Donna Isobel*

171

vaulted *mudejar* ceiling is adorned with the escutcheons of the seventy-two principal noble families of Portugal, each panel representing a stag bearing the respective family's crest between its horns. A blank space among these panels, once occupied by the arms of the House of Tavora, still bears witness to the fate of that unfortunate family, all the members of which were executed, and whose escutcheon was erased, by order of the 'enlightened despot', the Marquis of Pombal, following their alleged attempt on the life of King José I in 1758.

It was during the reign of King José's predecessor, Dom Joâo V (1706–1750), that the palace was considerably enlarged, and to this great builder are due the later wings and outcrops which further contribute to the external lack of symmetry and, being on various levels, inevitably add to the confusion of the internal lay-out. 'Almost every apartment', Beckford observed, 'has its vaulted passage and staircase winding up to it in a secret and suspicious manner.'

Almost every apartment likewise has its historical association, for Sintra never ceased to be inhabited right up to the end of the Portuguese monarchy. In one room, for instance, can be seen the fine mosaic floor fretted away by the ceaseless pacing of the mad king, Dom Afonso VI, who was dethroned and confined here for seven years by his brother and successor, Dom Pedro II (1667–1706). In a patio nearby stands the tiled seat on which Dom Sebastião sat to hear Camoëns read his *Lusiads*, that heroic epic of Lusitanian grandeur which encouraged the *exalté* young monarch to undertake, in 1578, the fatal expedition in Morocco that ended in his own death and led directly to the Spanish occupation of his country. The room next to the chapel contains a valuable ivory pagoda presented to Queen Carlota Joaquina in 1806 by the Emperor of China in gratitude for Portuguese aid in his campaign against the pirates of Malacca; and the bedroom of Queen Maria Pia of Savoy, the grandmother of the last king of Portugal, Manoel II, is still maintained in the state in which she left it when she fled from Sintra on the proclamation of the Republic in October 1910.

The existence today of these relics of the past is well-nigh miraculous considering the palace was almost totally destroyed during the great Lisbon earthquake of 1755. When Joseph Baretti, Secretary for Foreign Correspondence to the Royal Academy, visited it five years later, only three of its great halls were still to be seen, but 'they are rebuilding it', he noted, 'and the King will have it restored to its ancient form.'

The rebuilding was eventually completed, and since then the work of restoration has been regularly continued. The result is a striking tribute to modern Portuguese craftsmanship.

XAN FIELDING

172

The Chapel, probably built on the site of the original mosque

The Magpie Room, painted with birds holding the motto por

The mosaic floor of Afonso VI's bedroom, worn by his ceaseless pacing

A corridor with a typical mixture of styles

The King's Bedroom, its walls tiled with raised and coloured patterns of vine-leaves

The great topiary parterre is designed in the spirit of Le Nôtre

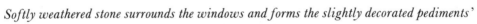
'Softly weathered stone surrounds the windows and forms the slightly decorated pediments'

Queluz

A rose-pink palace in the French eighteenth-century style

THE PALACE OF QUELUZ, near Lisbon, is elegantly rustic in a way that is very characteristic of Portuguese life and manners. It has a seductive grace, for its muted beauty grows on the beholder gradually, until at length the splendours of a more conventionally royal building seem almost vulgar in comparison.

The rose-pink colour-washed façade is cunningly designed with two low semi-circular wings springing out from a small central block. The southern side ends in a black onion dome above the chapel, and goes on at right angles in a series of dependent buildings of different sizes. The northern wing now contains a luxury restaurant in the original kitchens of the palace.

Softly weathered stone surrounds the windows and forms the slightly decorated pediments and the flambeaux set at intervals on the simple balustrade above. The vast, roughly cobbled space in front has always been a public highway and there is not even a railing to conceal the interior. But this is so with almost all the great houses and palaces in Portugal, for they are seldom set within parks, and are usually right in the middle of towns or villages. Queluz itself has recently become one of Lisbon's larger dormitory towns, but the palace, set in a slight hollow to the south-west on the way to Sintra, still seems remote, for the gardens and farmland behind also belong to the state, and in front there are only a few eighteenth-century houses and a strangely curved building where the royal servants were lodged.

Every major artistic movement in Europe reached Portugal a little late, as the country was, and in a way still is, cut off from the continent by the great land-mass of the traditional enemy,

Exquisite rather than magnificent, Queluz is an example of the Portuguese rococo, with two semi-circular wings springing out from the main block into a broad cobbled square

The formal approach to the palace is by wide flights of ingeniously graduated steps balustraded by elaborate statuary

OPPOSITE: Below the rose-pink façade is green foliage and the movement of water

The south front of the Robillon wing. The romantic upper part gives place to a severe Doric colonnade below

Spain. So it is not surprising that Queluz is one of the last great rococo buildings to be constructed in Europe.

Dom Pedro, son of the resplendent King John V, decided in 1747 to build a summer retreat in this secluded spot, which for over a hundred years had been the property of the second son of the reigning monarch. He called in Mateus Vicente de Oliveira who was soon joined by the Frenchman, Jean Baptiste Robillon. The latter was an extremely original designer, for his work under Ludwig of Ratisbon in the building of the gigantic classical convent-palace of Mafra, twenty years before, does not seem to have in any way affected the airy lightness of Queluz. His work is particularly notable in the garden façades and the interior decoration of the rooms.

A frenzy of activity, only broken by the necessity of sending a large number of the workmen to help in the rebuilding of Lisbon after the great earthquake of 1755, occupied the Prince and his architects. Fortunately the earthquake hardly affected the half-finished building. French artisans were sent for, stone came not only from the local quarries, but even from Genoa, wood was imported from Brazil, Denmark and Sweden, the ornamental marbles in the gardens were ordered from Italy and the lead statues were bought in England. Dr Ventura Porfirio, the curator, recently discovered that some of these are by John Cheere. There is a letter dated 1756 in the National Archives in Lisbon, signed by the then Portuguese Minister in London, Martinho de Melo, recording the purchase of ninety-eight lead figures for the sum of £871 17s. 1d. That was after the arrival of Dutch gardeners under the direction of Gerald van den Kolk who carried out Jean Baptiste Robillon's plans for the topiary gardens.

In 1760 Dom Pedro married his niece Dona Maria, who was heiress to the throne. They lived much in this palace, and later, when she had lost her husband in 1786, and become Queen, it was the scene of her attacks of insanity: her demented shrieks were heard by William Beckford during his visit to Queluz in 1794.

The interior of the palace is so light, elegant and beautifully furnished that the visitor feels that it could be lived in at any time; and this is indeed the case, for the Portuguese Government use Queluz for official entertaining.

Most of the rooms are quite small, with walls and ceilings painted in formal designs, the floors of polished red bricks, typically rustic and very cool in hot weather. One of the most original and exotic is the Sala das Mangas. It is long and narrow with windows on either side, for one of the peculiarities of Queluz is that it consists of a series of shallow one-storeyed wings of different sizes linked by higher pavilions. The whole room is lined with Chinoiserie glazed tiles, the *azulejos* so beloved of

A pair of splendid English lead figures of Roman nobles on each side of a doorway

Queen Maria I, the wife of Dom Pedro, whose religious mania developed into insanity

OPPOSITE

ABOVE: *The Hall of the Ambassadors by Robillon*
BELOW: *The Sala das Mangas, a long narrow room lined with chinoiserie glazed tiles in pale yellow and plum-coloured tones*

179

The King's Bedroom with a life-like bust of Dom João VI in a glass case. This part of the palace was restored after the fire of 1934

The Boudoir of the mad queen, Dona Maria I, containing panels of children dressing up in tricorne hats, by José Carvalho Rosa

Portuguese builders, which the visitor soon learns to accept and gradually to delight in. These are polychrome with blue and yellow tones prevailing over pale green and plum colours. A pair of ladies in formal eighteenth-century dress, one holding a huge branch sprouting strange flowers, the other with a sheaf of corn, stand at either end, and Chinese figures and curious birds and beasts are also depicted in these cool glazed panels.

The Sala dos Embaixadores is the throne room, but an intimate one, for the room is not very large and the windows on either side let in the sun, and the gardens and black and white marble floor are reflected in tall mirrors above the narrow semicircular console tables. This is the only room where the restoration after a great fire in 1934 appears obvious. The other rooms which were damaged have been admirably restored.

Beyond, at right angles, are the apartments of Dona Maria's son, Dom Joao VI and his sinister Spanish Queen, Carlotta Joaquina, whom Beckford described with such vividness. Sitting oriental fashion on a red velvet carpet laid on the grass, she made him run races with her ladies in the gardens and dance the bolero to a 'low, soft-flowing choir of female voices . . . smooth, well-tuned, and perfectly melodious'. The orchestra, which then existed at Queluz was, according to Beckford, the finest in

The Queen's Bedroom. It was from here that William Beckford could hear wild shrieks issuing during the last stages of the Queen's insanity

Europe and at that time the wooden theatre in the park still existed, though nothing now remains of it.

These end-rooms in the garden wing include the Queen's dressing-room with delightful panels of children dressing themselves up in tricorne hats and formal clothes by José Carvalho Rosa. The bedroom of the Queen, where she died in 1830, is very elegant in silver and nile green. There is an unusual, almost life-size, wax bust of the King, Dom João VI, in his bedroom, cruelly depicting his pendulous jowls and unattractive face.

In the Sala das Merendas, however, we get away from the influence of that unhappy royal pair, for this is a wholly enchanting room surrounded by canvases of a *fête champêtre* by Joao Valentim. But this is a Portuguese picnic. The gaily clad figures sit on the ground talking and laughing, white cloths are laden with chickens, bread and fruit, while sporting dogs insert questing noses into the corners of the pictures and waiting horses are silhouetted in the background.

On the other side of the entrance hall, the rooms are lined with silk with painted ceilings. The fine furniture includes a pair of beautiful red lacquer screens and sets of Portuguese Hepplewhite and Chippendale chairs. Oriental and European porcelain stand on the tables and there is a remarkable life-size bust of

A detail of the Ballroom. The ceiling is supported by gilded caryatids in the Louis XV style

One of a pair of superb chandeliers in the Ballroom at Queluz

LEFT: *The Ballroom, magnificently decorated by mirrors and gilded boiserie*

Dona Maria I from the Rato factory in one of the rooms. Giovanni Ender's portrait of the flashing-eyed Dom Miguel, the adored son of Carlotta Joaquina, indicates how inevitable it was that he should become involved in the wars of succession after the Royal Family had returned from Brazil, where they went on the arrival of the French in Lisbon during the Peninsular War. Finally there are two splendid oval rooms, the music-room with an Empire grand piano and the ball-room with mirrors set slightly out from the walls and golden caryatids supporting the ceiling, from which hang a pair of superb chandeliers. The rooms beyond the ball-room are not shown at the present time, which is to be regretted, as there is an unique gun-room frescoed with trees and foliage in the manner of Pillement, with hunting scenes adorning the ceiling.

The chapel was the first part of the palace to be finished, for it was opened for worship in 1752. It is a lovely, rather dark, rich ensemble of gold rococo wood work picked out in tango red, green, pink and blue. One of the royal galleries above contains a small organ case, notable for its fine rococo detail, and in the

QUELUZ

chapel is an extraordinary portable font with a marble basin set in a highly decorated frame with a gilt carved wood cover.

The gardens are also rustic, in that they do not attempt to emulate the formal eighteenth-century gardens in France, for they were designed by Robillon for a country palace in a country setting. The overpowering scent of box fills the upper garden from where the artful irregularity of the palace can best be seen, with its Chinese roofs and false windows. Fountains and pools with lead, marble and stone figures are set in formal box-edged beds and there are a pair of really splendid English lead figures of noble Romans outside the central doorway. At the end of these topiary gardens, an oval fountain is backed by a pair of Italian marble sphinxes with pie-crust ruffs round their necks.

In the lower part of the garden there are pools and fountains set in tall thick hedges of yew and cypress, and alleys of magnolias and mulberry trees (planted by General Junot when he lived here during the Peninsular war) leading to the great double staircase going down from the highly ornamented garden wing. In front is the Dutch canal, made of *azulejos*, one of the most unusual features of the place. There is a stream running through it, but the sluice gates are only shut in the month of

The Music Room, constructed in 1759 but re-designed in 1768, is distinguished for its oval ceiling and chandeliers

The Gun Room, frescoed with trees and foliage, and hunting scenes on the ceiling

May, so that then the water comes up to the edge of the blue and white tiled pictures of shipping scenes with which the upper part of the confining walls are lined, and Robillon's fantasy can be seen as he envisaged it; later in the year the stream dries up and earlier there is danger of floods. On the exterior the canal walls are composed of more formal tile scenes in lilac, set in polychrome frames. Below this canal is a kind of skittle alley, now much restored, but which is contemporary with the palace and above it a further canal bordered with Chinoiserie tiles. Hidden away on the other side of these canals, past a strange shallow octagonal pool with rococo crimped edges, is a fountain which has been attributed to Bernini. The tritons and dolphins, weathered to a lovely hue, may well be by him, but the central figure is thought to be from another hand.

Queluz is a rewarding place, for it is gay and filled with light, and memories of the mad Queen Maria I and her sinister daughter-in-law, Carlotta Joaquina, no longer cast their shadows over this pale pink palace where they lived. Rather it is the great beauty of the irregular façades and the superbly unobstrusive way in which the house and gardens are maintained, that the fortunate visitor will recall.

SUSAN LOWNDES

Tsarskoe Selo

The magnificent palace of the Empress Catherine the Great

An eighteenth-century engraving of the Hermitage, one of the many elaborate pavilions in the garden of Tsarskoe Selo

OPPOSITE: *Onion domes rise above the elaborate façade at the extreme end of Rastrelli's building*

186

TSARSKOE SELO – the village of the Tsars – now called Push-kino in honour of the poet who spent his adolescence and wrote his first poems there, is not its original name. Up till 1725 it was called 'Sarskoe Selo' – the village of Saari – derived from the Finnish name *Saari mois*, meaning 'an elevated spot'. It is in fact situated on a hill, and the climate is very much more mellow than that of St Petersburg.

It was first referred to in 1702, when the Swedes, pursued by Russian troops, retreated to Saari. The battles that took place in the Neva basin led to great devastation, and it is by pure chance that the hamlet of Saari was spared.

By 1710 the danger from further attack by the Swedes had subsided, and Peter the Great made a gift of it to his future wife, Catherine. As her country estate it soon became Tsarskoe Selo, the village of Tsars. The future Catherine I, a woman of austere taste, commissioned the German architect Braunstein to build her a modest palace of stone, surrounded by a Dutch garden. She succeeded Peter the Great in 1725 and became ruling Empress until her death in 1727. After the accession of the Empress Elisabeth, daughter of Peter the Great, in 1741, the building was to become the battlefield of two opposing tastes and temperaments, a tribute to two remarkable women, both empresses of the eighteenth century, the Empress Elisabeth and Catherine the Great. Elisabeth, voluptuous, lascivious, flamboyant, dreamt of eclipsing the splendour of the Court of Louis XV. The palace was first reconstructed on a relatively modest core by the Russian-born architect Kvassov. But the Empress was content only

when her chief architect, Count Bartolommeo Francesco Rastrelli, *Il Magnifico*, totally rebuilt it between 1749 and 1756 in the most sumptuous rococo style. Rastrelli was for Elisabeth what Lebrun was for Louis XIV. In him she had found the man she wanted, an architect who was trained in France, Italy and Central Europe, an eclectic in the best sense of the word with the rare ability to combine elements from other styles without becoming wholly derivative. His genius left its mark on Russian architecture of the middle years of the century, and in fact it was due to his imagination that a special brand of Russian rococo, Elisabeth's rococo, came into being.

The palace was of unparalleled magnificence. A forecourt enclosed by two quadrants leading to two pavilions connected by a monumental central gate, framed right and left by green lawns, exalted its approaches. Today one can only guess at its original splendour. All the ornaments of the façade, the pillars, caryatids, now painted in a dark brown, were at that time either white or gilded. A balustrade ornamented with statues and golden urns ran along the roof. The people, in their näivety, believed that the whole roof was of massive gold.

Elisabeth was intensely proud of her Tsarskoe palace and liked to boast of it to distinguished visitors. They were all dazzled by it. Only one stranger, perhaps of more discriminating taste or of a less sycophantic turn of mind, dared to declare that the palace was disproportionately long and that its architecture was heavy. The abundance of gold seemed to him in bad taste. He was not wholly wrong. The proportions of the great palace at Tsarskoe Selo are even more overwhelming than those of the Winter Palace, and this dramatic façade, burdened with ornament, gives the impression, as do most of Rastrelli's buildings, of an ephemeral theatrical décor. Nowhere else does one become so aware of the profound influence of the theatre on eighteenth-century architecture. The interior decoration has, alas, suffered greatly from the fires of 1820 and 1863 and most of all in the Second World War.

The staircases were decorated by murals – the work of Hubert Robert, the French painter of romantic landscapes with classical ruins. One of these murals represented the Gallery of the Louvre, lit from above, and another the imaginary ruins of the same gallery. The state apartments, which adjoin one another, overlook the main forecourt. First comes the famous Amber Room (*iantarnaia komnata*) with its walls completely panelled in amber, pale as honey. It had been made specially for the King of Prussia, Friederich Wilhelm I. Peter the Great saw it at Monbijou when he was in Berlin in 1717. The sergeant-king agreed to surrender it to him 'in exchange for eighty tall recruits'.

On the other side of the main staircase is the Silver Room, where all the ornaments and furniture are of plated silver. The

Catherine II of Russia, known as Catherine the Great, in 1762. She did not share the Empress Elisabeth's taste for flamboyant architecture. She created at Tsarskoe apartments where she could live in privacy

OPPOSITE: *Not even a Chinese summerhouse is out of place in the huge park of Tsarskoe Selo with its frequent changes of mood*

TSARSKOE SELO

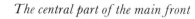

The central part of the main front

The palace extends for over a furlong

The palace after 1945, before its restoration

The steps to the pavilion built by Cameron for Catherine II

The main entrance with the monogram of Elisabeth on the balcony

The work of two empresses and two architects

Catherine the Great's bedroom, with its slender pillars and wedgwood plaques

One of Catherine's private rooms which were remodelled for her by Cameron

The ante-chamber to the chapel decorated in blue and gold

The Green Dining-room with a vista through to the other private apartments

191

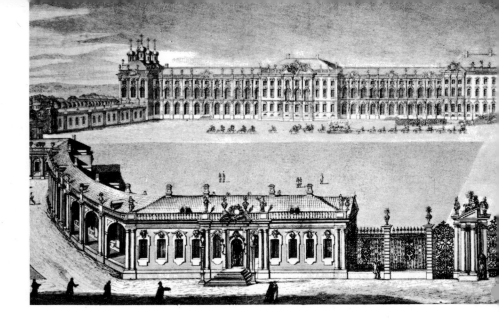

A portrait of the Empress Elisabeth

The fireplace in the Blue Dining-room

Great Gallery, built on the designs of Rastrelli, vies with the Versailles Galerie des Glaces. It is sixty-seven *archins* (the *archin* is about thirty inches long) in length and has thirteen front windows. All the panels between the windows are covered by mirrors, beautifully framed in gold.

We then come to Catherine the Great's period of influence. She had a special weakness for Tsarskoe, where she spent all her summers after 1763. But Elisabeth's pomp and display were not to her taste. In St Petersburg she had a Hermitage built for herself beside the Winter Palace; here in Tsarskoe she wanted private apartments where she could live in absolute privacy. For this transformation she turned to John Cameron, a Jacobite and a Scot, a great architect steeped in antiquity, a lover of the classical style so dear to Catherine's heart, and author of a book on Roman baths. Cameron – who lived in Rome in the house of the Pretender – whose taste was shaped by Palladio and Clerisseau, was to introduce into Russia the neo-classicist Adam style. He totally transformed the right wing of the palace. Rastrelli's wide stairs were sacrificed to the Chinese Salon, two antechambers were demolished to make room for the Salon de Lyon, the walls of which were entirely covered with striped yellow silk. Catherine's private apartments include the Silver Room where she listened to the reading of official reports, and a row of rooms, the delicate decoration of which is inspired by arabesques from Pompeian frescoes. The bedroom is adorned with small pillars in violet-coloured glass set in bronze and with Wedgwood plaques encrusted in the walls. The Blue Room, the only one that had preserved its original furniture, is papered in a milky green with a golden design, the doors framed in small blue glass pillars, and gives the effect of a valuable snuffbox, as it was indeed nicknamed. Catherine was delighted with the Pompeian rooms. 'I confess', she wrote to Grimm in 1782, 'that I've been here for nine weeks and never stop being fascinated by my surroundings. My Quarenghi says that it is both beautiful and modern but you can't visualise it until you've seen it.'

Up to then only slight alterations of Elisabeth's palace had been carried out. But from 1779 to 1792 Cameron executed a

A general view of the huge palace in the eighteenth century. Today it is impossible to obtain this overall vista owing to the surrounding woods

gigantic plan of reconstruction that included the Agate Pavilion, the colonnade and a slope descending to the park. The Agate Pavilion consists of a round toilet-room, of the jasper study and of a large salon where rose marble mingles with white. Most of the medallions and bas-reliefs are the work of the French sculptor Rachette. The colonnade is reached from the park by a monumental staircase and bronze busts of great men from antiquity adorn the space between the pillars. In this company it is surprising to find a bust of Fox. 'With his eloquence he had prevented England from making war on Russia,' the Empress said. 'I have no other way of expressing my gratitude,' and she placed him between Demosthenes and Cicero. 'Pitt will be jealous,' she added. The gentle slope was added by Cameron when Catherine, as she grew old, found it hard to manage the steep stairs. Cameron superimposed classical purity and a noble restraint on the baroque lavishness of Rastrelli. But his style was far from austere and he made generous use of precious materials, marbles from the Urals, silver and bronze. Yet his interiors were not as ostentatious as Rastrelli's rooms with their rococo splendour; they had the same quiet elegance as the country houses built by the Adam brothers in England.

Later on the greatest architect of Catherine's reign, Giacomo Quarenghi, who arrived in Russia in 1780, was also employed at Tsarskoe Selo. He designed a residence for her grandson, the future Emperor Alexander I, and in 1795 he reconstructed Catherine's Silver Room. During the Second World War the enemy destroyed this resplendent work of art. They systematically demolished the furniture, mutilated all the ornamentation, cut out the encrustations and pillaged all the valuable pieces that had not been evacuated in time. Two fires, in 1942 and 1944, did the rest. What remained of the past splendour were some parts of the Great Hall and a few rooms adjoining the church.

After the war, restoration work began. The surviving fragments were carefully collected as models. Today, what has been a dream for so long is slowly becoming reality.

MOURA BUDBERG

The Green Dining-room was one of the first rooms to be designed by Charles Cameron for Catherine the Great. It is decorated with neo-classical reliefs

The Winter Palace

A masterpiece by Italian and French architects on the Neva

A corner of the Winter Palace seen from across the River Neva as the ice floes were breaking up

IT IS IMPOSSIBLE TO TALK of the Winter Palace without first conjuring up a picture of the city of St Petersburg, now Leningrad, and of the Neva River. I know of nothing in the world more beautiful than that great expanse of limpid and tremulous water, purified by the filter of the Ladoga Lake, and constantly agitated by tiny iridescent waves, that flow impetuously between the double dam of its magnificent embankments built in the rose granite of Finland. And the powerful stream that moves between the golden needle of the Petropavlovsk Fortress and the long façade of the Winter Palace is but a very small part indeed of the great river.

After the Neva, what strikes every visitor to St Petersburg is the overall immensity of scale. The whole city has been built, it seems, with the magnificence of the Neva in mind. There is an architectural unity about it. It has style. That is why those who criticise the dimensions of the Winter Palace should, I think, look back at the history of the city's development through the years and at the different mentalities of its rulers.

Nothing remains of the first Winter Palace built for Peter the Great in 1711 in his favourite Dutch style on the site of the Hermitage Theatre, shortly after the foundation of the city in 1703. This was a modest two-storied building with a slate roof that looked out on the canal linking the Neva with the Moika River. The canal took the name of Winter Canal, or rather Winter Dyke (Zimniaia Kanavka) from the name of the palace. The second palace was built in 1721 by the German architect, Georg Johann Mattarnovi, who came to Russia with Andreas Schlüter,

The palace seen from the Triumphal Arch. In the centre of the square rises Alexander's Column

The side of the palace away from the Neva

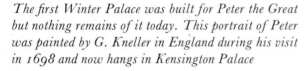

*The first Winter Palace was built for Peter the Great
but nothing remains of it today. This portrait of Peter
was painted by G. Kneller in England during his visit
in 1698 and now hangs in Kensington Palace*

the architect of the Royal Palace in Berlin. This building looked
out on to the Neva itself and was still on the modest side. In
fact it was also a two-storeyed house but with a central projecting pediment supported on pilasters and with a rusticated basement. Peter the Great died there in 1725.

St Petersburg was growing rapidly. Peter the Great, who
favoured northern architects, summoned the Swiss-Italian architect, Domenico Tressini, who prepared the first plans for the
Cathedral, for the monastery, the Alexander Nevski Lovra and
the Cathedral Church of St Peter and Paul. In order to link the
Admiralty with the monastery a large avenue was planned with
the name of 'Grand Perspective' – the future Nevski Prospect.

It was also Domenico Tressini who rebuilt the Winter Palace
and doubled its size and reduced Mattarnovi's façade to the
status of an end pavilion of a more luxurious building.

The Empress Anna Ioannovna, when she returned to St Petersburg in 1732, after the capital had been transferred to Moscow
during the short rule of Peter II (1727–30), moved from this still
unassuming palace to the neighbouring and infinitely grander
house of Count Apraxine. It was she who commissioned the
Italian architect Count Bartolommeo Francesco Rastrelli to re-
design the Winter Palace by incorporating in the new building
another house from the northern side of the Palace Square. This

ABOVE: *The palace which we see today is its final form after four re-buildings, each to an increasingly large scale. The front facing the Neva is 100 feet high and over 500 feet in length*

LEFT: *The palace, built in 1721 by Mattarnovi. Peter the Great died there in 1725*

BELOW: *The Neva in the eighteenth century, with the Winter Palace on the right, as it was re-built for the third time by Tressini*

The palace is a reminder of Russian links with western Europe

The Winter Palace is now part of the Hermitage Museum and was restored after the fire in 1837

RIGHT: *The Main Staircase, formerly known as the Ambassadors' Staircase, is one of the few parts of the palace retaining its original eighteenth-century style. The huge columns of grey granite were added in the middle of the nineteenth century*

ABOVE AND LEFT: *The Pavilion Hall of the Small Hermitage as it is today was the work of A. Stackenschneider (1802–65). The Small Hermitage was originally built by Vallin de la Mothe in 1764 and was used by Catherine the Great both as a museum and a refuge from her Court duties. Monolithic columns support a light gallery decorated with lace-carved railings. On the right of the lower picture is the famous Peacock Clock which was made by the Englishman, James Cox, and purchased by Prince Potemkin*

The Western-European Silver Room in the Hermitage

The 'Gallery of 1812' built by C. Rossi in 1826 to commemorate Russia's victory over Napoleon

was the fourth version of the palace. After the accession of the Empress Elisabeth, Rastrelli continued to alter and increase the dimensions of the Winter Palace and in 1753 he presented the Empress with an entirely new plan. The plan was accepted and work began on a scale hitherto unimaginable. The new palace was ready in 1759, shortly before Empress Elisabeth's death, but changes went on until 1768 and later, well into the nineties, when the work of Starov and Quarenghi, employed by Catherine the Great, gradually began to alter the character given to the interior of the palace by Rastrelli, except for the church and main staircase that remained unchanged. Work in the palace continued in the nineteenth century when Karl Ivanovich Rossi, the architect who is mainly responsible for the grandiose town planning of St Petersburg, built a gallery for the heroes of the 1812 war which was immortalised in a poem by Pushkin. Now the Winter Palace and the Hermitage are one, and both the state and private rooms are integrated into the Museum.

With Catherine the Great in power we find a new style creeping into the character of the buildings, classical tendencies from the West replacing Elisabeth's Russian rococo style, the Palladian influence reaching as far as St Petersburg. The town gradually became, particularly in the reign of Alexander I, an 'Empire' town; its classicist features were introduced first by Quarenghi and later maintained by Rossi. Rinaldi, the Italian architect, and the French Vallin de la Mothe, both employed by Catherine the Great, brought the Louis XVI style to St Petersburg, but on an overwhelming scale, inspired and required by the gigantic dimensions of the Neva.

The actual building of the Winter Palace has the shape of an elongated rectangle. The two principal façades – on to the Palace Square and on to the Neva – are completely open to the view, while the lateral façades are concealed, one by a garden created in Nicholas I's reign, behind high granite walls, the other by the Hermitage pavilion. The palace is 100 feet high and over 500 feet in length, yet owing to the over-abundance of ornament it produces the impression of an opera décor. Rastrelli had planned it to be painted orange, with the ornaments in white, but when it was damaged by fire in 1837, in the reign of Nicholas I, and restored by the architects Stassov and Brullov, it acquired a red-brick colour. Today it is painted a pale green with the details in white, which lightens the whole aspect very favourably and reduces its theatrical quality.

The interior of the palace (the exterior was faithfully reconstructed), which contains 1,500 rooms, was only partly restored after the fire of 1837 to look as far as possible like the original. The state rooms are a fairly correct replica, while the rest is considerably changed. So it is, in fact, a palace of the nineteenth century inspired by a model in rococo style. But the famous

Jourdain staircase, which the Tsars descended on every Epiphany when proceeding to the ceremony of the blessing of the waters of the Neva, has remained intact in its truly imperial grandeur. The Room of the Order of St George, where the First Douma was opened, had Corinthian pillars in white marble. The Peter the Great Room, where diplomats used to foregather on New Year's Day to offer their good wishes to the Emperor, had pillars of jasper and furnishings of red velvet embroidered with double-headed eagles. The Nicholas Room, with sixteen windows overlooking the Neva, used to be the scene of court balls. There are beside these the White Room with marble statues of antique gods, the Alexander Room devoted to the war of 1812, the beautiful Malachite Room, the Arabian Room and many others.

The Winter Palace was richer in beautiful pieces of furniture than in works of pictorial or sculptural art, though there were a few busts by Rastrelli's father, Shubin, and some portraits by Nattier, Roslin and Vigée-Lebrun.

On the second floor is the Treasury Room, containing the Romanov Regalia and the private rooms of the Sovereigns, restored by Brullov after 1837.

It was Jean Jacques Rousseau, the apostle of the simple life, who gave Catherine II the idea of building a Hermitage beside the Winter Palace, as in fact there was one already in Tsarskoe. It was Vallin de la Mothe who built the pavilion, which was linked by a gallery to her other apartments. It was there she frequently entertained her intimate friends, Diderot and Grimm. The rule for those who crossed the threshold was to 'leave their dignity at the door, together with their hats and swords'.

In 1905, after the revolution, Tsar Nicholas II left the Winter Palace in the same way as Louis XIV abandoned the Louvre for Versailles, for Paris always held for him memories of the *fronde*. But the Tsar did not move to Moscow. He established his residence in Tsarskoe for the summer, in the Crimea for the winter. While living in the Winter Palace the Russian Tsars continually saw their burial places – in the Peter and Paul Fortress – from their windows. Perhaps it was a tragic presentiment that drove Nicholas II away from that view.

In the October Revolution of 1918, the Winter Palace was stormed by detachments of red army sailors and soldiers. They entered by the main entrance on the Palace Square and established themselves in the Malachite Room.

In the Second World War the Palace suffered greatly from artillery fire, and particularly from dampness as most windows were smashed by the explosions. Restoration began immediately after the siege of Leningrad came to an end and has now almost been brought to a successful completion.

MOURA BUDBERG

The statue overlooking the Main Staircase, which was the grandest of the 117 staircases in the palace

A stucco panoply in the Guard Room

The Royal Palace
MONACO

A Mediterranean fortress transformed into a gracious house

THE PALACE OF MONACO was erected on the site of an old fort built by the Genoese in 1215 which had merely consisted in four towers connected by ramparts. The south side, overlooking the sea, was left unfortified. Each tower was four storeys high and was topped with a flat roof surrounded with battlements. Three of them faced eastward, towards the town, while the fourth guarded the opposite side.

In 1297, François Grimaldi, of noble Genoese stock, captured the castle. He was, however, unable to hold it and the castle changed hands several times more. At last the Grimaldis gained a decisive victory. They were able to hold their position, settled in Monaco and established their dynasty there. They were daring sailors, too, and their glory shone in many naval battles. In 1304 the King of France, Philippe le Bel, appointed Rainier Grimaldi, Rainier I, Admiral-General of France. His son, Charles I, captured Monaco and enlarged the castle by adding two new main buildings, one against the eastern ramparts and another looking out over the sea on the south. These new buildings changed the appearance of the citadel. It was now more like a fortified house than a keep. During the second half of the fifteenth century Lambert and John II adorned the main wing with loggias and in it they placed the State Hall, an important room where the princes of Monaco carried out their official functions. This Hall is now known as the Guard Room.

The Genoese, however, could not accept the loss of such an important stronghold. In December 1506 they sent an army with heavy artillery to besiege Monaco. The town was invaded

ABOVE: *The Tour de l'Horloge (left) and the Tour de l'Oreillon. The latter is one of the four towers built by the Genoese in the thirteenth century*

OPPOSITE: *The great white palace of the Princes of Monaco is a construction of many different periods, with the Genoese fortifications as a platform for the eighteenth-century palace*

A portrait of Louise-Hippolyte, Princess of Monaco, by Vanloe (1712) showing the palace of Monaco in the background

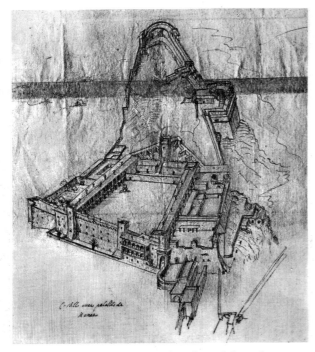

An early seventeenth-century drawing of the palace

OPPOSITE: *On the north and south sides of the palace old cannon and mortars are placed alongside pyramids of large cannonballs*

but resisted fiercely. When the final assault was made on March 19, 1507, the besiegers gained a foothold on the ramparts but were finally repulsed by the defenders and the siege was lifted. It had lasted 102 days. After repairing the buildings that had been damaged by the shelling, Lucien I turned his attention to the castle. He added to the main wing by erecting what was to be known as the Ercoleo, a name derived from the frescoes with which the walls were covered depicting tales from the *Legends of Hercules*. Augustin I again increased the size of the living quarters in the palace. He was thus able, in 1529, to give a state reception to the Emperor Charles V who spent four days in Monaco on his way to Italy to be crowned by Pope Clement VII.

The palace again acquired a different aspect under Honoré I (1532–1581). It was he who commissioned Dominique Gallo, a Milanese architect, to add two storeys of arcaded galleries along the south wing, known as the State Rooms Wing, and had frescoes painted by Luca Cambiase, a Genoese, along the opposite façade. It was probably then that galleries were added along the north wing that looked over the harbour approaches.

A very accurate early seventeenth-century drawing, which is reproduced here, allows us to have a clear picture of what the castle then looked like. The old towers and battered walls, together with the crenellated parapets and powerful bastions surrounding the buildings, give to the whole a rugged appearance that is somewhat softened by Lambert Grimaldi's loggias and by the galleries added by Dominique Gallo.

There were three towers along the main wing where the lords lived: St Mary's Tower, the Middle Tower and the South Tower. To the right a round building guarded the entrance to the castle, for military strength was still its main purpose. As artillery improved, the art of defence was modified to meet the new threat. Honoré's new system of defence was based on two main points, All Saints Tower and the Serravalle Bastion. The first, of semi-circular shape, guarded the end of the rocky promontary. It had a platform for guns and was connected to shelters, hacked out of the rock, in which cannon were also placed. Underground passages connected it with the Serravalle Bastion, which consisted of three storeys of vaulted casemates, and which was likewise armed with guns.

It was Prince Honoré II (1604–1662) who transformed the castle into a palace. Its forbidding aspect was modified by adding decorative embellishments to the main façade. New buildings, including a chapel surmounted by an elegant cupola, closed the west side of the main courtyard, while the finishing touches were put to the wing containing the State Rooms by adding to it a magnificent suite of drawing rooms.

Honoré II laid out a French-type garden on the side facing the sea and adorned it with a charming summer-house. This

LEFT: *The palace of Monaco in 1732 by the Mona-gasque artist, Joseph Bresson. This view was made from nearly the same direction as that of the drawing reproduced on page 204 done a century earlier, and shows the changes made by Prince Honoré II*

summer-house, known as the Bath Pavilion, is reached by going through an arcaded porch, decorated with statues, which leads in to a suite of rooms. There is an elliptical swimming pool in the largest room, surrounded by figures of gods and goddesses set in niches. These works were all carried out under the direction of the Genoese architect Jacques Cantone. Another Genoese artist, the painter Orazzio Ferrari, adorned the first-floor balcony of the state rooms by frescoes of *The Labours of Hercules*. It was he who painted the big fresco that covers the ceiling of the Grimaldi Room (now called the Throne Room) showing an incident from *The History of Alexander the Great*. All state ceremonials have been held in the Throne Room since the sixteenth century, and here it is that fealty is sworn at the accession of each Prince.

Prince Honoré II assembled a huge and valuable collection of

The Rocher de Monaco overlooking the port and the Mediterranean. The large building in the centre background is the famous Oceanographic Museum, founded in 1906 by Prince Albert I

OPPOSITE: *The Mazarin Room with the portrait of Cardinal Mazarin, chief minister to the young Louis XIV. The room is decorated with polychrome boiseries of the seventeenth century*

A strong fortress softened by loggias and charming courtyards

A corner of the main courtyard

The main entrance in front of which stand two members of the Monagasque Guard

The gracious double colonnade of the Cour d'Honneur

The main staircase, modelled on the horseshoe staircase at Fontainebleau

works of art. Among other items mentioned in the inventory made after his death are seven hundred paintings reputed to be work of the greatest masters, but mention need only be made here of several portraits by Titian, of which one was of Charles V and another of the Prince of Valdetare.

Honoré II was succeeded by his grandson, Louis I. He it was who had a huge doorway made in the main frontage of the palace, topped by a pediment bearing the princely arms. He also constructed a great twin marble staircase in the main courtyard; the harmony of its line is reminiscent of the staircase built in the courtyard of the palace of Fontainebleau by the architect Jean du Cerceau. The architrave of the new door and the flight of steps in the main courtyard were both designed by Antoine Grigho, an architect from the region of Como.

Prince Louis I was famous for his prodigality and when he visited England in 1677 and spent some time in London, he vied with the English King Charles II in the bounteous gifts he showered upon Hortense Manzini of whom both he and Charles were enamoured.

Prince Antoine I further embellished the so-called Royal Room. He commissioned the Genoese painter Gregorio de Ferrari and Alexandre Haffner from Bologna to paint a figure of Fame on the ceiling and to place figures of the Four Seasons in the lunettes.

Louise-Hippolyte, Antoine I's daughter, her husband Jacques I and their son Honoré III but rarely visited the Principality. Honoré happened to be there, however, when illness forced King George III of England's brother, Edward Duke of York, to land at Monaco in 1767. He was received at the palace and died in the Royal Bedchamber, known since then as the York Room. George III, in return for the Prince of Monaco's hospitality, invited him to visit the English Court. This he did the next year and was granted the honours due to a sovereign.

The palace was a splendid place at the end of the eighteenth century. Unfortunately it did not escape the fury of the French Revolution. France annexed the Principality of Monaco on February 14, 1793. The furniture and the beautiful art collections in the palace were soon put up for auction and the buildings were used as barracks and then served as a poor house.

The palace was in a dreadful condition when the Principality regained its independence. The Bath Pavilion was in such bad repair that it had to be demolished. The work of restoration was started under Honoré V and finished by Prince Charles III. The latter rebuilt St Mary's Tower, placed a new altar in the chapel and had its vaulting covered with frescoes. On the façade the frescoes of Jacob Froëschle and Deschler depicted the past glories of the Grimaldis and of the Principality. Finally the Guard Room was completely altered. A huge chimney-piece

The York Room in which Edward, Duke of York died in 176

The elaborate overmantel in the Throne Room

...nirror in the York Room

was inserted and the whole was decorated in renaissance style.

Prince Charles III also endeavoured to reassemble the collections that had been scattered by the French Revolution. Thanks to his efforts and to those of his successors, a fine collection was again acquired. Among the great masters whose works are hung in the state rooms and the private rooms are the portrait of Lucien I by Ambroggio de Predis; that of Honoré II by Philippe de Champaigne; the head of Antone I, by Hyacinthe Rigaud; the portrait of Jacques I, by Nicolas Largillière; of the Princess Louise-Hippolyte by J. B. Vanloe; of Honoré III by Louis Tocqué; of Prince Albert, the learned oceanographer, by Léon Bonnat; and finally of Prince Louis II, the present Ruling Prince's grandfather, and of his mother, Princess Charlotte, painted by Philip de Laszlo de Lombos. In addition to these family portraits there are subject pictures and allegorical or mythological scenes: for instance, *The Music Lesson*, a picture painted by Titian as a young man; *A Woman Doing Embroidery*, thought at first to be by Holbein and then ascribed to G. Ströts; a charming oil painting by François Lemoyne, *Venus Dressing*; and one of Louis Lagrenée's best paintings, *Love's Education*.

Prince Louis II applied himself to making a collection of things that had belonged to Napoleon. His interest in this was due to the fact that his mother, Princess Mary, *née* Douglas-Hamilton, was the grand-daughter of Stephanie de Beauharnais, Grand-Duchess of Baden. This collection of Napoleon's personal possessions contains one thing of particular interest, namely the flag belonging to Napoleon's Battalion of Grenadiers at Elba. The collection also includes some arms with engravings by Boutel, some silver-ware bearing the mark of the well-known silversmith Biennais, some orders that are but seldom seen and finally some touching mementoes of the king of Rome. The collection also includes a set of coins struck by the Princes since the first half of the eighteenth century, some important historical documents, and a library with shelves of old book bindings with armorial bearings. Lastly there is the Stamp Museum founded by Rainier III. This not only contains the old postal ciphers but the different stamps used in Monaco since 1854.

His Most Serene Highness Prince Rainier III is continually improving and modernising the palace while leaving its historic character unimpaired. Since his accession the paintings have been restored, the suites of rooms have been refurnished and the decoration has been renewed. He started the custom of holding splendid summer concerts in the wonderful setting of the main courtyard. In short, thanks to Their Most Serene Highnesses Prince Rainier and Princess Grace, the traditions of the great eras live on and this wonderful place of residence has recaptured its ancient grandeur.

ALBERT LISIMACHIO

211

ABOVE AND BELOW: *Two views of Schönbrunn by Bernardo Bellotto (1720–80). The upper picture shows the rear of the palace from the rising park and the lower one, the main courtyard. The buildings on each side of the courtyard were later removed or altered*

Schönbrunn

The palace which symbolizes the peak of Viennese maturity

SCHÖNBRUNN is perhaps the most exalted monument ever to be erected to that famous national characteristic of the Austrians – their *Gemütlichkeit*, or easy-going cosiness. For over 200 years, together with the Hofburg in the city centre, this palace in the western suburbs of Vienna was the main seat of the Hapsburg dynasty, and thus the centre of all the Austrian history that the world remembers. Yet, unlike its great architectural and political rivals, Versailles and Potsdam, it remained also a home. Despite its size (there are no fewer than 1,441 rooms in the building), and the sumptuousness of its galleries and state apartments, something of this domestic aura clings even to the untenanted palace of today.

The homely note is struck at once by its low, almost sprawling lay-out. Only a modest balustrade, enclosing five extra top windows on the courtyard side and seven on the garden side, marks the centre of the edifice. Otherwise the central and side tracts are of the same height and the same decorative emphasis, while the wings, by being thrust unobtrusively forward, seem both to embrace the entrance and to beckon the visitor towards it.

This suggestion of envelopment is repeated in the front outer staircase, which curves down from the main gallery in two crooked arms to the ground; while, on the garden side, another semi-circle of steps leads with equal informality direct from the balcony of the ceremonial apartments on to the lawns. Above all, there is a welcoming warmth radiating from the sheer rich colour of the building – the famous 'Schönbrunn yellow', imitated in hundreds of country houses and thousands of cottages

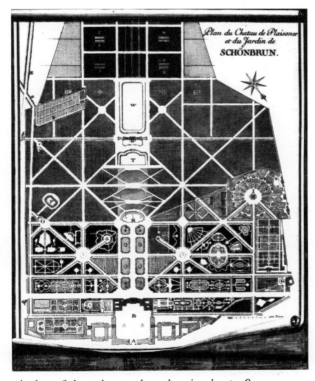

A plan of the palace and gardens in about 1800

SCHÖNBRUNN

wherever the old Empire stretched, from the Alps to the Carpathians and from the Polish steppes to the lagoons of Venice. Schönbrunn was, and is, a lovable as well as a beautiful building.

Architecturally, it has a curious history. The ground on which it stands, the so-called *Katerberg*, first came into the hands of the Hapsburgs in 1569 when the Emperor Maximillian acquired it, partly, it seems, to house the exotic private zoo of camels, apes and elephants he had brought with him to Vienna from Spain and the New World. The original royal hunting-lodge built there was razed to the ground by the Turks in 1683 during their last vain siege of the Austrian capital and twelve years later the Emperor Leopold determined to construct upon the site a summer residence that would be the talk of Europe and the envy of her courts.

The architect selected was Johann Bernhard Fischer von Erlach, already the acknowledged master of Austrian baroque, who produced a plan worthy of his Emperor's ambition: a series of five great ornamental terraces which ascended the gently sloping field and led up to an immense series of buildings along the crest of the hill, more monumental in scale and magnificence than anything the Empire had seen.

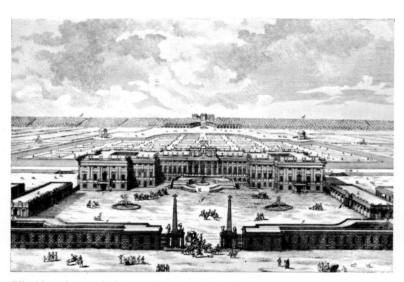

The 'hunting and pleasure' schloss in about 1750

The garden front in 1784

The thirty-seven Ionic pilasters of the main façade were each topped by a statue, and it remains much as Von Erlach designed it

This plan doubtless took the Emperor's breath. It threatened also to take all his money, and Fischer von Erlach was commanded to design something rather less awe-inspiring.

Fortunately for the comfort of the Hapsburgs, his second and more manageable plan was immediately approved and work on it duly began in 1696. The original gigantic terraces were replaced by a formal sloping garden (which Jean Trehet was brought from France to design) and the palace itself was brought down to the hollow of the so-called *Wiental* instead of being perched up on the windy crest.

The three-storeyed structure of the amended plan was virtually complete by 1713, though final alterations (by Nicolaus Pacassi) were not carried out until 1749. Pacassi did his share towards stamping the imprint of a country house on this imperial palace; it was he who tore down the three domes which Fischer von Erlach had erected over the central tract and replaced them with the flat 'top storey' described above. The tall Ionic pilasters which von Erlach had placed between each of thirty-seven window sections, as well as the statues which sat on the balustrade exactly above each pilaster, were, however, left untouched, as was the rest of the original outline.

Baroque decoration, especially in a Hapsburg residence, could never be a simple art form, and the interior of Schönbrunn is a great deal more elaborate than the clean low-slung lines of its exterior might suggest. The show piece is the Great Gallery which runs along the entire length of the central portion on the courtyard side, linked by open indoor archways to the Small Gallery, running parallel with it on the garden side. Here is baroque in all its disciplined magnificence – richly inlaid wooden

A distant view of the Gloriette monument from the stairway on the garden front

LEFT: *The Gloriette monument, which crowns the park that rises at the rear of the palace*

OPPOSITE:

ABOVE: *The Blue Room, decorated with Chinese motifs and Chinese genre paintings in the oval and rectangular wall-panels*

BELOW: *The circular Chinese Room contains this large porcelain vase surmounted by a dragon. It is an eighteenth-century Japanese work*

The Great Gallery

Here is baroque
in all its disciplined
magnificence

The Hall of Mirrors on the main floor

The baroque theatre, one of the finest in existence

A fireplace in the 'Hall of Ceremonies'

floors, cream and gilt panelling, glittering crystal chandeliers and wall brackets, gold ornamented stucco work at every turn and the whole richly balanced scene crowned by three ceiling frescoes of Gregorio Guglielmi depicting Austro-Hungary in war, the arts and the sciences.

Yet, once away from the Great Gallery – whose impressiveness was, so to say, obligatory upon the dynasty – a note of intimacy manages to creep in again. True, many of the smaller rooms lack nothing in extravagance: the 'Million Room', for example (so named because it was supposed to have cost a million thalers) which is a dazzling vision of inlaid rosewood and 'wallpaper' of rare Indian miniatures on vellum. But the prevailing atmosphere in these minor apartments is of gaiety rather than of pomp. With the aid of a few comfortable armchairs, either the Pink Room, the Yellow Drawing Room, or even the Emperor Franz Josef's spartan bedroom could be lived in as they are today by ordinary mortals without suffocating.

For this atmosphere Schönbrunn must thank, more than any other of its illustrious tenants, the Empress Maria Theresa, who moved into the palace in 1746 and lived there with her large family through most of the summers of her long reign until her death in 1780. Maria Theresa was a wife and a mother almost before she was an Empress, and she took Schönbrunn in hand accordingly. Under her, Pacassi toned down the façade; the park was re-laid, being criss-crossed with dead-straight avenues to give frequent glimpses of the palace; the Botanical Gardens were laid out (at the plea of her consort, Francis I); the famous

The 'Hall of Ceremonies', adjoining the Great Gallery. In the centre is the portrait of the Empress Maria Theresa who lived in the palace for many years

'Gloriette' triumphal arch, the Obelisk and the Roman Ruins were all erected in the grounds; and finally, the little Palace Theatre, itself a gem of late baroque, was built.

This Palace Theatre, incidentally, was once the scene of an incident which typified the informal way that Schönbrunn was run under its homely Empress. One evening, in 1768, she burst into her box in the middle of the performance to announce the birth of a precious grandson – stopping both actors and audience dead in their tracks by bellowing out excitedly: 'Children, Poldi (Leopold) has just had a boy!'

From the day that Maria Theresa took up residence, Schönbrunn became, of course, the seat of Hapsburg power as well as the hearth of the Hapsburg family. Thus, throughout the last two centuries of the Empire's life, it saw both the noonday splendours and the long death agony of the dynasty.

It was here that Maria Theresa, with her famous Chancellor, Kaunitz, planned the defence of her possessions in war and peace against the claims of Bavaria, Saxony, France and Prussia. It was here, in 1805 and again in 1809, that Napoleon took up a conqueror's residence in Vienna – leaving, as souvenirs, the two French eagles which still squat on the entrance gate. It was here, after his defeat, that many of the festivities of the Congress of Vienna were held in 1815, when Schönbrunn became the splendid setting for a diplomatic settlement which was to give the old Europe of the Emperors its last full generation of peace and stability. It was here, in 1830, that Franz Josef was born; here that he lived during the sixty-eight summers of his record-breaking reign and also died, in the middle of the First World War that brought both the old order and his own dynasty down in ruins. Finally, it was here, in November 1918, that Emperor Charles, signed the Act of Renunciation from State Affairs which ended six hundred years of Hapsburg rule in Vienna.

The palace went on to share the tribulations of the Republic as well. In February 1945, 270 bombs fell on the building during two Allied air raids on the German-held capital; the central tract was severely damaged and one of Guglielmi's frescoes destroyed beyond repair. But the work of restoration began even while the palace was still being used as the headquarters of the post-war British occupation forces (a tenancy in which the writer shared for eighteen months – installed with more luxury than comfort in an Archduchess's bedroom).

By 1951 the palace was again as Maria Theresa would have wished and, since Austria regained her freedom in 1955, it has done its best to look as modest and as neutral as the second Austrian Republic itself. Without much success, for the Austria that *it* symbolises was neither.

GORDON BROOK-SHEPHERD

A mirror in the Hall of Mirrors

The front façade of the Upper Belvedere overlooking the main courtyard

The north side of the Upper Belvedere with one of the many garden fountains in the foreground

The Belvedere

A palatial but infinitely graceful achievement of baroque

IF BAROQUE IS GLORIOUS SUPERFLUITY, then Vienna's 'garden palace' of Belvedere is its supreme symbol in Austria, for the main building, or Upper Belvedere was never meant to be lived in at all. The whole of this massive cream and gold extravaganza, straddling the crest of the park, was created simply as a stage setting for audiences and receptions. One slept somewhere else – usually in its equally handsome but more modest twin, the Lower Belvedere, which nestles at the foot of the gardens, half a mile down the slope.

There is something else symbolic about the place. The man who built it and first inhabited it (the word 'lived' is somehow inadequate) was Prince Eugene of Savoy, the famous general of three Hapsburg emperors and comrade-at-arms of Marlborough. And it was his victories in battle which made Austrian baroque, his own Belvedere included, possible.

For baroque along the Danube was not just a style of art, or even a whole form of culture. It was a way of life – an exuberance in dress, speech and manners as well as in stone; and this exuberance sprang from relief that the dangers which had so long threatened the Empire's existence were at last banished. In 1683, Prince Eugene's rescue army drove the Turkish janissaries from the gates of Vienna, saving Europe as well as Austria. His further triumphs in the field put the Turks to flight for good, leaving the black double-eagle of the Hapsburgs unchallenged throughout the Danube basin. Henceforth silk could be worn, not armour; palaces could be built, not castles.

In 1693 Prince Eugene started to plan his own, by buying up

Above the entrance to the Upper Belvedere is the coat-of-arms of Prince Eugene of Savoy who built the palace

The Lower Belvedere seen from the rear, or garden, side. This was built in 1714–16 and was the actual residence of Prince Eugene

a cluster of pasture lands called *Zum Lampelbrunn* which sloped up from the Rennweg, and from the top of which he could see those Vienna woods down which he had led his soldiers ten years before to save the beleaguered capital.

The Prince took as his principal architect a former engineer officer in his army, Johann Lukas von Hildebrandt (1668–1745), who, with Fischer von Erlach and the Tyrolean Jakob Prandtauer, makes up the giant trio of Austrian baroque builders. Hildebrandt, of German blood, came up from Italy where his inspirations had been Carlo Fontana and Palladio. In the Belvedere, he created for his master and for posterity a rare blend of Teutonic solidity and Mediterranean caprice.

The lower palace, and actual residence, was built between 1714 and 1716. It provides the only breath of ordinary humanity in the whole complex. Indeed, if the phrase is conceivable in connection with Prince Eugene or Hildebrandt, it is what a baroque bungalow would have looked like had one been built.

The lines are deep and horizontal, the basic structure is single-storeyed and, despite the statues which crowd the parapet of the central two-storeyed section, it has about it an air of simple modesty, as if it hardly dares to raise its eyes at its huge relative up on the crest. The high sloping roofs, whose red-brown tiles are the perfect foil to the yellow of the walls, emphasise this bungalow air; even more than the lineal façade which runs below them, these five separate roofs seem to bind together the centre block and the wings, each with their corner pavilion.

Inevitably, since we are in one of the temples of baroque, this impression of ground-hugging homeliness disappears the moment we step inside. True, the arrangement of rooms in the main tract is simple – a straight row looking out on to the gravel courtyard of the garden. But the decoration has all the ornate disciplines and rich colour harmonies of the period – the deep red of the marble flooring and columns, the cream and gilt of the porcelain stoves that once struggled to warm all this luxury, and the dead white of the statues and the stucco work. The pinnacle of this intimate extravagance is the so-called 'marble hall' with ceiling paintings by Altomonte, whose strong, saturated colouring sets off all the varied tints of stone and enamel below.

The name 'garden palace' was not bestowed for nothing: the slope which stretches from the Lower to the Upper Belvedere is an integral part of the design. The exact squares of lawn, bordered by gravel paths; the tall hedges, trimmed with razor edge precision; the fountains with their pouting naiads; the grey, blank-eyed sphinxes which squat on the terrace steps; the granite vases, from which cascades of stone fruits and flowers hang forever suspended – all this is not a living garden so much as a sculptured carpet laid out between the two buildings and locking them together.

The garden front, by Soloman Kleiner, c. 1731–40

Kleiner's engraving of the principal façade

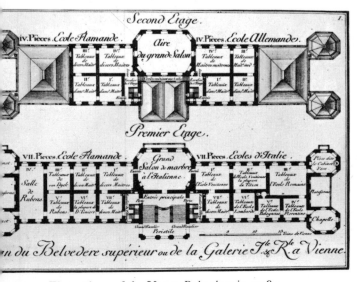

Floor-plans of the Upper Belvedere in 1781

The climax to Hildebrandt's creation, the Upper Belvedere itself, was completed in 1721–22. The great building is in seven sections, three-storeyed at the centre and two-storeyed at the flanks, where the four corners are each rounded off with an eight-sided pavilion with cupola. In the Lower Belvedere, the south in Hildebrandt's artistic soul won over the north. Here, at least in the outside aspect, it is the north which prevails over south. The massiveness of the Upper Belvedere is its main characteristic, and neither its perfect proportions nor the elaborate motifs carved on all the window recesses, cornices, parapets and friezes can quite relieve this feeling of solemn weight. It is a splendid matron of a building rather than a radiant young woman; and only when the matron looks at her reflection in the artificial lake on the courtyard side does she seem to shed a little of her plumpness in the water.

However, Italian gaiety has much more to say on the inside, as the names of some of the many artists responsible for the frescoes and wall paintings testify – Carlo Carlone, Gaetano Fanti, Santino Bussi, Francesco Solemena and Giacomo del Po. None is an artist of commanding fame, yet none is of less than first rate merit. Perhaps that is why, working as a team under Hildebrandt's inspired direction, they produced one of the finest blends of baroque interior decoration to be found anywhere in central Europe. A typical example of this blending is the central double staircase in white marble, whose heavy square balustrade is perfectly set off by groups of rounded cherubs supporting wrought-iron lanterns twice their size (a favourite device of Hildebrandt's, and one that he repeated in the staircase of the Daun-Kinksy Palace only a mile away).

The lavish series of inter-connecting apartments which run the length of the main first floor were all designed to be stood in rather than sat in. The eye is dazed by so much splendour – as indeed it was intended to be – and selection becomes difficult. But, in the north-west wing, the white stucco marble room with its rich gilding is perhaps the finest while, in the opposite north-east wing, pride of place must certainly be given to the so-called Gold Cabinet, with its tall doors and carved pilasters, all in gold leaf, and the intricate patterns of inlaid wood which cover the floor.

In the Upper as in the Lower Belvedere the *pièce de résistance* is the central Marble Chamber; and, for the main building, Hildebrandt reproduced his smaller pattern in twice its size and splendour. The basic tone is a shade heavier, for the Corinthian wall columns, the door surrounds and the fireplace as well as the flooring are all predominantly of rich red marble. But, once again, this solemnity is to some extent balanced by those cherubs and goddesses who sit, without talking to each other, on painted pedestals beneath the domed roof; while the sheer

225

Under Hildebrandt's direction artists enlivened the interior

The lower hall of the Upper Belvedere, a splendid achievement of baroque decoration

Groups of cherubs support Hildebrandt's iron lanterns   *The double staircase of the upper palace in white marble*

RIGHT: *A garden sphinx, straddling a distant view of the spire of St Stephen's Cathedral in Vienna*

BELOW LEFT AND RIGHT: *The garden statuary in the Belvedere is conceived in the same baroque style as much of the interior*

height of the room, which runs up right through the central tract of the palace, gives it a certain lightness. All in all, even those parts of the Belvedere which Prince Eugene intended should take our breath also succeed in charming our eye.

The history of the palace, at least under the Empire, was a sad one. It was as though its first owner, by building an edifice not designed for human habitation, had laid a curse on all who attempted to live in it afterwards. When, in 1736, Prince Eugene died (not even in the Lower Belvedere but in his town palace, the present Austrian Finance Ministry) there was no son to carry on. His cousin and heiress, the Princess Viktoria von Sachsen-Hildburghhausen, ran through the great man's fortune as fast as she could squander it. In 1752, only sixteen years after his death, his garden palace of Belvedere was sold to the Hapsburgs.

The star-crossed dynasty had an even unhappier tenure there. It was in the Upper Belvedere, for example, that, in April 1770, the Archduchess Maria Antonia took her farewell from Vienna at a splendid court gala before leaving the palace to become the bride of Louis XVI. Twenty-three years later, as Queen Marie Antoinette, she met her death with him on the scaffold.

After one hundred years ghostly existence as an Imperial picture gallery, a new Hapsburg tenant moved in, the Archduke Franz Ferdinand, heir to the Austrian throne and political rival of his uncle, the Emperor Franz Josef. It was from the Belvedere that, in July 1914, Franz Ferdinand and his morganatic wife, Countess Sophie Chotek, set out for their state visit to the southern crown lands of the Empire – the journey that was to end in their assassination at Sarajevo and the start of World War I.

Not until after the Second World War was the 'jinx' on Belvedere banished. In May 1955 the palace was the scene of one of the happiest events in Vienna's history, the signing, in the Marble Chamber, of the treaty that brought freedom and independence to the Republic after seventeen years of foreign occupation. It was a moving moment to witness when the great crowd of Viennese, packed solid on the lawns and gravel paths, cheered themselves hoarse as the red-bound treaty, with the ink of the statesmen's signatures barely dry, was waved from the open balcony. One felt that Prince Eugene, who had himself liberated Vienna 273 years before, would have forgiven the severe damage being inflicted by the 'common people' on his precious gardens.

GORDON BROOK-SHEPHERD

LEFT: *A detail of the stairway hall, illustrating 'one of the finest blends of baroque interior decoration to be found anywhere in central Europe'*

Huis ten Bosch

The elegant 'House in the Wood' of the Dutch Royal Family

An early eighteenth-century drawing by V. Klotz of the Huis ten Bosch

Professor Th. H. Lunsing Scheurleer's extensive article, a 'Reconstruction' of the rooms used by Amalia van Solms, (grouped round the Orange Zaal) around the year 1650, will be published in Oud Holland 1969 no. I

THE SEVENTEENTH CENTURY represents one of the most interesting periods in the architectural development of the northern Netherlands. The Dutch had challenged the Spaniards for their freedom, but it was not until the reign of Frederik Hendrik, a son of Prince William of Orange, that Holland attained political and cultural unity.

The Princes of Orange had at first been modest in their residential requirements. Frederik Hendrik, however, after assuming the Stadholdership in 1625, ushered in a new period and began his architectural activities by rebuilding the old castle at Honselaarsdijk, soon to be followed by the Huis ter Nieuburch at Rijswijk and the wings of het Oude Hof (the Old Court) in the Noordeinde at the Hague. Finally, the Oranjesael or Huis ten Bosch ('the House in the Wood') was planned by Pieter Post at the wish of Princess Amalia van Solms-Braunfels. Countess van Solms, a maid-of-honour at the court of Frederik V of the Palatinate, had married Frederik Hendrik of Orange in 1625.

It was in May 1645 that the Directorate of Finance of the County of Holland issued a decree by which a piece of land of about fifty acres on the north-east side of the Hague was ceded to Princess Amalia van Solms. It is from the correspondence of the Prince's secretary, Constantyn Huygens, that a good deal is known of the building operations. Devised as a summer residence or country pleasure-house, the building was turned by Princess Amalia into a mausoleum to the memory of her husband, who died in 1647, just before the palace was completed.

The architect was Pieter Post, but the painter-architect Jacob

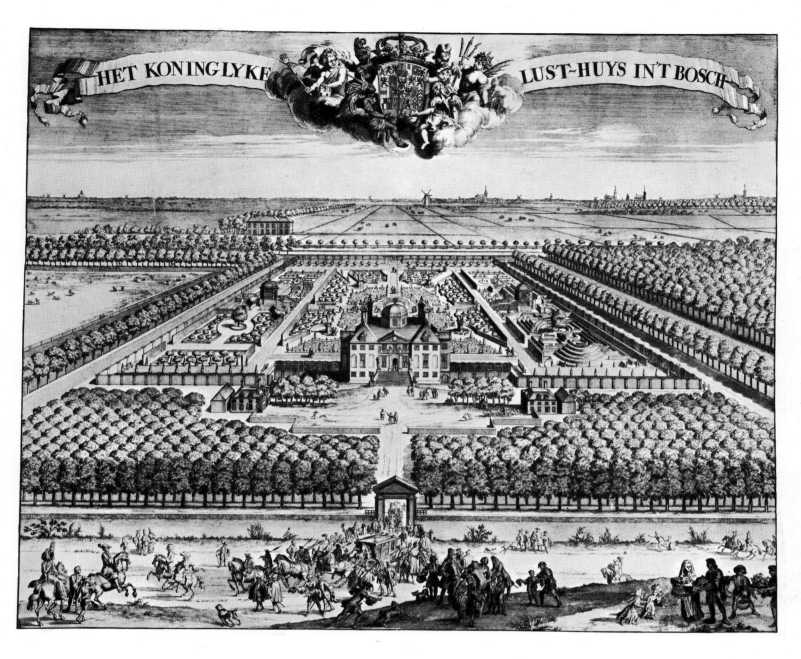

HET KONINGLYKE   LUST-HUYS IN'T BOSCH

ABOVE: *A late seventeenth-century engraving of the Huis ten Bosch. At that time it was known as the Oranjesael in memory of Frederik Hendrik of Orange, who died in 1647*

LEFT: *The Huis ten Bosch by Jan van der Heyden (1637–1712), who was the first painter in Amsterdam to specialise in architectural subjects*

The central part of the palace, which was the original building, seen from the garden

OPPOSITE

ABOVE: *The Huis ten Bosch from the west. The Japanese Room is situated above the colonnade*
BELOW: *The main entrance to the palace with its large outside staircase* (stoep) *and the two wings added by Daniel Marot*

van Campen was put in charge of the final plans. The house is symmetrically planned in the manner of a Palladian villa, and its main feature is a central hall which takes up most of its height. In consultation with Huygens and Count Johan Maurits of Nassau, a number of painters were invited to assist in the decoration of the interior. Huygens suggested that the house should be called 'de Oranjesael', the Hall of the House of Orange, and it was he who devised its symbolic scheme to record the prince's glory.

The engravings of Pieter Post (1655) and Jan van der Groen (1668) show the delicate structure to advantage. The château was modest in size and was flanked on both sides by additional buildings. The garden, designed by Post, was composed of a *parterre* of small plots devised along rigid symmetrical lines and acted as a setting for the house. From *groene kabinetten*, or gazebos, the visitor could overlook the garden with its royal emblems embedded in the *broderies de parterres*. Jan van der Heyden (1637–1712) drew a charming picture of the ensemble, showing the

garden side of the house. The two square out-houses are just visible beyond the trees, and obelisks and urns on wooden posts divide the *parterres* from the kitchen garden. Statues, raised high on pedestals, face each other in straight lines near the house.

Princess Amalia died in 1675, and it was her daughter, Princess Albertine Agnes, who relinquished the Orange Hall to her nephew Prince William III, the future King-Stadholder. The new owner celebrated the occasion by a ball, and the state reception was officially recorded by Daniel Marot, the Huguenot artist and craftsman, who accompanied Prince William III to England as his chief architect. Commissioned by Prince William IV to enlarge the Orange Hall on the occasion of his marriage to Princess Anne of England, Marot added two wings. His task can have been far from easy. The main building dominates. The front façade has an enlarged *stoep*, or flight of steps, and projects outwards, the whole effect emphasized by the contrasting use of natural stone and brick. At the same time the silhouette of the octagonal dome and lantern was changed. On the garden side, sash-windows open on to a balcony, and a flight of steps links the house with the garden. Indoors little remains of Marot's work, but his taste and sense of proportion can still be recognised in the White Dining-room. Four *grisailles* by Jacob de Witt (done between 1738 and 1748, the fourth added much later) and a Waterford crystal chandelier complement the famous domed ceiling, which Marot executed towards the end of his life.

Next to the dining-room, with its rococo *hollandais*, comes the Chinese Salon. The interior was a gift to Prince William V from a Mr Hemmingson, once a senior merchant in the service of the United East Indies Company in Canton. It has a wallpaper painted with scenes of the cultivation of rice, and the embroidery on the curtains and furniture, and the Chinese paintings on the

Detail of a wall in the Chinese Room

Embroidered peacocks in the Japanese Room

OPPOSITE

ABOVE: *The Chinese Room. The interior decoration was a gift to Prince William V from a Far-eastern merchant*
BELOW LEFT: *The White Dining-room*
BELOW RIGHT: *The Waterford crystal chandelier in the White Dining-room, seen against Daniel Marot's famous ceiling*

LEFT: *The Blue Salon with beechwood furniture and portraits by unknown artists of the daughters of Frederik Hendrik and Amalia van Solms and their children*

235

A detail of the Oranjesael. The portrait is of Amalia van Solms with her daughters, by Gerard van Honthorst

OPPOSITE: *Part of the Oranjesael. The doors on the left depict Minerva and Hercules opening the doors to a figure representing Peace. The painting is by C. van Couwenberg*

A view of the garden side of the Huis ten Bosch in the eighteenth century by P. C. La Fargue

The monogram of Frederik Hendrik and Amalia

mirrors, are enchanting. Equally interesting is the Japanese Room, with rosewood panelling inlaid with lacquer, completed in the late nineteenth century by mural decorations in embroidered silk and damask depicting flowers and exotic birds. The stucco ceiling, with its evenly spaced decorations painted in black, has Chinese details in the corners.

The French dominance between 1795 and 1815 swept aside the old way of life. Prince William removed his family to England for safety's sake, and the palace underwent many changes. Used successively as a lodging, prison, national art-gallery, a museum open to the public, official residence of the State Pensionary Schimmelpenninck, temporary dwelling of Louis Napoleon and Governor-General Lebrun, the Oranjesael acquired the name of *het Palys in het Bosch*, 'the Palace in the Wood'.

It was after the return of the House of Orange in 1813 and the accession of William I as constitutional monarch, that the palace, although at the disposal of the King, became the property of the Netherlands State. In use by three successive kings, the House in the Wood became the favourite summer residence of Princess Sophie of Wurtemberg, William III's first wife. A renowned linguist and patron of the arts, her guest-book, which was laid open every day in the Oranjesael, contains the names of such eminent men as von Humboldt, Ranke, Liszt, Macaulay, Renan, Morley, Thiers and Lord Clarendon. At the

An eighteenth-century view of the Huis ten Bosch from the entrance gates, by P. C. La Fargue

beginning of the nineteenth century, Zocher Senior designed the curving landscape garden. It may well be that these gardens lacked subtlety, but they had other qualities. Flowers returned to the garden, and with flowers, colour and scent, while seclusion was an added attraction. We have come a long way from the rectilinear pattern of the Dutch countryside, yet the garden has a quite undeniable charm.

Queen Wilhelmina repeatedly mentions the Huis ten Bosch in her book *Eenzaam maar niet Alleen*. In 1899 she made it available for the first World Peace Conference. During 1950–56, the palace was completely restored. Self-contained flats were built in it for the Princesses, and air-conditioning and central-heating installed, without changing its character. Great care was taken too in the choice of furniture, wall-decorations and *objets d'art* to give each room a stylistic unity. The garden, a present from the Dutch people, was partly laid out in the old manner along symmetrical lines. An old gateway, another present, was erected at the entrance on the side of the Leidsche straatweg, and now stands sentinel to the park.

Today Queen Juliana's permanent home is the Soestdijk Palace, but the Huis ten Bosch is frequently occupied by the Royal Family both for private visits and state occasions.

C. M. CREMERS

A punchbowl in the Rijksmuseum decorated with views of the Huis ten Bosch (above) and a synagogue (below). It is made of Hague porcelain, c. 1774

Tullgarn

A charming lakeside summer-palace of the Swedish monarchy

The courtyard facing the sea, with steps leading down to the jetty

OPPOSITE: *Tullgarn lies on an inlet of the Baltic with a view out over the skerries*

MUCH OF SWEDEN IS composed of very wild country, and even today one can travel for miles through the rock-strewn, dark pine forests only occasionally seeing a cluster of houses or a gang of wood-cutters or a school bus on its daily round, returning the children from the school-house in some local township. Every now and then one comes to a town which has grown up round the timber industry, but such towns are mostly fairly new and it is hardly an exaggeration to say that in the seventeenth and eighteenth centuries there was nothing but wilderness stretching over most of Sweden – dark, terrifying and, it is easy to imagine, filled with trolls and other supernatural beings. Separated by these vast forests, were the three principal areas of habitation. The most important was around Stockholm, and stretched some seventy miles inland to include the cathedral and university city of Uppsala, and the iron-mining towns to the north. The other two areas consisted of the hinterland of Göteborg (Gothenburg), and the more hospitable southern part of the peninsula, which was mainly agricultural. With a few exceptions, Sweden's country houses are found concentrated in these three areas. Those in the south are associated with great estates, while those around Göteborg were chiefly the retreats of the rich merchants and shipping-magnates of that city. Those in the Stockholm area, on the other hand, were the country seats and summer residences of the Swedish nobility, who needed to be within the reach of the Court and the capital.

Many of the country houses round Stockholm lie in the most idyllic surroundings, often on one of the many lakes which, in

'It is only a moderately large country house'

An engraving by Ulrik Thersner, 1825

summer, are usually dead still, their waters only broken by the diving of a great-crested grebe or the rising of a fish. Others are situated on the shores of some inlet along the rocky coastline, looking out over the low, grey skerries to seaward. It is on such an inlet that Tullgarn lies, with the Baltic lapping the shore at the bottom of its garden. Strictly speaking, Tullgarn is not a great palace at all. It is, in fact, only a moderately large country house, but it has been the much-loved summer residence of several members of the Swedish Royal Family.

The present building was erected in the 1720's by Magnus Julius de la Gardie, a member of a powerful Swedish family of Dutch descent. For this work he employed a Frenchman named Joseph-Gabriel Destain. Destain had served as a military engineer in the Swedish army, but when the war with Russia finally came to an end in 1720, he found himself out of a job and with a considerable amount of back pay owing as well. So he joined the de la Gardie household as a secretary and then seems to have tried his hand at architecture, in which field he was strongly influenced by Nicodemus Tessin. Destain built a handful of other houses in the neighbourhood as well. They are all much alike – pleasing, straightforward buildings of no very special merit but set in what, at any rate in summer, is a smiling landscape.

One approaches Tullgarn through this pleasant countryside and enters the castle grounds through a gateway in outbuildings lying some distance in front of the main building but arranged on its central axis. From the gateway the drive leads straight to the house through a glorious double avenue of lime trees, the remains of the old baroque garden. An old map shows that the drive was originally flanked by fishponds and that in the woods to either side lay various small buildings – a brewery, stables, an orangery, an ice-house, a pavilion and a smithy. At the back of the house, the courtyard faced the sea and a path led down to a jetty and a boathouse. An inventory drawn up in 1733 gives one

OPPOSITE

ABOVE: *The approach to Tullgarn between the double avenues of lime trees, which are the survivors of the old baroque garden. The balcony and window surrounds are alterations but the façade is essentially that designed by Destain in the 1720's*
BELOW: *Tullgarn in spring seen from across an arm of the Baltic*

an excellent idea of how such a Swedish country house was furnished. It was only the state rooms that were decked out with any degree of magnificence and the finest room of all was the King's Bedroom (the de la Gardies had, of course, to receive royalty every now and then), which had a set of Lille tapestries on the walls and contained a handsome French bed with watered silk hangings trimmed with silver lace. The other state rooms had only painted imitation-tapestries, although in each there were one or two fine pieces of furniture – a Venetian mirror, a japanned and gilt table, a glass chandelier – and all the rooms had window-curtains which were still comparatively rare at that time. Most of the chairs were stiff and upright, but Her Grace had a single easy-chair covered with a brightly-coloured plush. This was about the only concession to comfort in the house. The poor daughters of the household had very bare rooms upstairs and, even though most of the rooms had stone floors (for fear of fire), several had no stoves or other means of heating. This contrast between the splendour of the state rooms and the extreme simplicity of the rest of the house is a striking feature of many of the older Swedish country houses.

Tullgarn's history as a royal residence begins in 1772 when the house became the property of the King, Gustavus III, who immediately put it at the disposal of his younger brother, the Duke Frederik Adolf. The Duke was apparently a man of excellent taste and the changes which he instituted at Tullgarn turned it into a charming place, no doubt very different from the dark, northern baroque home of the de la Gardies.

First, the building was altered in various ways: another storey was added to the wings, the roof was rebuilt and a new staircase was provided because the old ones allowed smells from the damp cellars to creep up into the house. But, for all this, the exterior of the house does not appear to have been changed in any very radical way. The interior, on the other hand, was completely redecorated in a light, unoppressive neo-classical style. This decoration, applied to the well-proportioned rooms of the old baroque mansion, has produced a very pleasant amalgam. It has recently been restored in an exceptionally sensitive manner and the effect is delightful.

Frederik Adolf had visited Italy, as all high-born young men of his day were expected to do, and had brought back with him more than a passing enthusiasm for classical art and decoration. On his tour, he also acquired a number of books on the classical antiquities (one of them was a present from the Pope), and these were in several instances a source of inspiration for the artists who executed the new decorations in his house.

The Duke could, of course, make use of the services of the court architect and his assistants, and it is clear that sketches for some of the principal alterations came from this quarter. Much

The Red Ante-chamber, with a handsome fire screen

Writing desk and filing cabinet by Nils Dahlin

The Small Ante-chamber, decorated by Hultgren
OPPOSITE: *A corner of the white and gold State Bed-chamber. The medallions have a ground of simulated porphyry*

The Entrance Hall, redecorated in the late nineteenth century. The whole is tiled with a miscellaneous collection of Dutch tiles

ABOVE RIGHT: *The State Bed-chamber. The charming and delicate decoration was probably designed by Jean Baptiste Masreliez and was executed in the 1790's*

of the decoration seems to have been composed by an artist of French extraction named Jean-Baptiste Masreliez who was a talented exponent of a graceful and airy kind of neo-classicism. In this work he was assisted by various Swedish artists and craftsmen including a certain Anders Hultgren, a painter who had struggled through the Stockholm Academy and who was therefore judged capable of composing and executing whole sections of decoration on his own. Hultgren was no genius but, when working under the direction of Masreliez, he was able to produce some perfectly acceptable work. Left to himself, on the other hand, he tended to stray from the narrow paths of the academic canon and mix his styles, so that among his classical figures and formal arabesques, one suddenly finds naturalistic animals, birds and flowers taken straight from the artist's own Swedish countryside. The effect is strange but it is this very lack of archaeological precision in Hultgren's work, coupled with the informality of Masreliez's decoration, that make the neo-classical embellishments at Tullgarn so much less tedious than those, for instance, at Haga, which was Gustav III's own neo-classical pavilion, or those in so many similar interiors elsewhere in Europe.

The redecoration of Tullgarn dragged on through the last years of the eighteenth century and was not quite finished when Frederik Adolf died in 1803. They were completed by the time his sister, Sofia Albertina, took up residence there in 1807. She used the house as a summer retreat and kept going, deep into the nineteenth century, a household that was a relic of the *ancien régime* (she died in 1829). There is a charming description of this milieu by one of the Princess's ladies-in-waiting, a young woman with the splendid name of Ebba Oxenstierna af Eka och Lindö. The house was filled, she tells us, with flowering plants

LEFT: *The alcove in Duke Frederik Adolf's Bed-chamber. The bed bears his coat-of-arms*

BELOW: *Part of a cupboard dated 1571*

and bushes; everywhere there were little work-tables on which lay pieces of unfinished embroidery; in the old billiard room now stood a piano and open on it lay music by Rossini and Weber, while in Her Royal Highness' bedroom was a small shelf with a select little library including works by Sir Walter Scott, Madame de Sévigné, Madame de Staël, Grimm and Sismondi. Miss Oxenstierna was probably right when she wrote: '*Que l'on savait ici non seulement pàsser le temps, mais aussi l'employer et que ce n'était pas l'aiguille seule qui charmait les loisirs de ces lieux.*'

In the 1880's, Tullgarn was modernised and became the home of the prince who was later to become Gustav V, and of his wife, Princess Victoria of Baden. Several of the rooms were now re-decorated in what one authority has called the 'German *biers-tube* renaissance' style, complete with dark panelling, heavy shelves, balusters, grotesque details, antler-chandeliers, and the rest. The staircase was hung with examples of Swedish peasant weaving – bright-coloured tapestries with rather simple patterns – and bedecked with copper and pewter vessels of various kinds. The result was oppressive, but it is worth remembering that it was out of this kind of interest in peasant art and in the tradi-tional craft-culture of the countryside that the modern Swedish talent for applied art grew. The interest shown in high places for such work must have been a potent and encouraging in-fluence on this development.

Gustav V died in 1950 and Tullgarn has not been used since then, although it still belongs to the Crown and is a private house. Recently, however, it has been opened to the public during the summer.

Detail of a stove of Swedish faïence tiles in the Small Ante-chamber. Late eighteenth century

PETER THORNTON

ABOVE AND BELOW: *Two engravings by Jean Eric Rehn, after drawings by Palmcrantz, of the Royal Palace at Stockholm in the mid-eighteenth century. The upper drawing is of the east façade, and the lower one of the east and north façades. The statues on top of the building were never erected*

The Royal Palace
STOCKHOLM

One of the finest examples of French taste outside France

THE SWEDES MUST HAVE FELT they were well on the way to becoming a great Continental power at the end of the seventeenth century. Already, during the Thirty Years' War, Sweden's small but well-trained armies had distinguished themselves in central Europe under the leadership of their king, the dynamic Gustavus Adolfus. A quarter of a century later, Gustavus X had beaten the Danes by yet another stroke of brilliant generalship. This defeat did not finally settle the long drawn-out quarrel between the two countries, but it forced Denmark to give up the fertile southern part of the Swedish peninsula. By this accession, Sweden was at last confined within her natural borders, and had at the same time added to her own small population the industrious peoples of the southern provinces who had long enjoyed a comparatively advanced state of civilisation and many close links with the Continental mainland. During the seventeenth century Sweden also consolidated her hold on various territories on the other side of the Baltic – notably in Pomerania, which involved her in German politics, and in Finland, which brought her into close contact with Russia. All this meant that Sweden came to be regarded as a potent force in the politics of northern Europe, a nation which the major European powers now found it well worth their while to try to enlist as an ally.

In 1687 an energetic Swedish architect named Nicodemus Tessin (the Younger; his father, of the same name, was also an architect) visited Versailles in the course of an extended study-tour and was there fired with a deep admiration for the whole elaborate apparatus with which Louis XIV was enshrining the

The entrance on the north front. These regal gateways are in contrast to Nicodemus Tessin the Younger's more severe style in the other parts of the exterior, which reveal the influence on him of the Italian late renaissance and baroque styles

249

The entrance to the Palace Courtyard

concept of Absolute Monarchy. On his return to Sweden, Tessin lost little time in trying to persuade his own King, Charles XI, that he too must surround himself with a degree of splendour in keeping with the exalted and powerful position that the King of Sweden now occupied. Charles was at first reluctant but since he was, after all, an Absolute Monarch and since he really rather liked magnificence, he was finally persuaded to play the role that Tessin had mapped out for him.

The first and most obvious requirement at this point was to provide the King with a decent palace. This was not so easy. The then existing Royal Castle in Stockholm was a somewhat ramshackle medieval fortress with various more or less successful renaissance additions. Tessin drew up plans for some major alterations to this confused mass of buildings and, early in the 1690's, the work of tidying up the old castle was started. He can, of course, never have expected to turn the castle into anything approaching Louis XIV's conception of what a palace suitable for a seventeenth-century monarch should be like. Tessin must have been delighted when, on May 7, 1697, the old castle burnt down. By this stroke of fate, the whole situation was

OPPOSITE: *The centre of the south façade, bearing traces of Nicodemus Tessin's admiration for Caprarola and the Pitti Palace*

The west façade, mostly dating from the end of the seventeenth century. The herms, dating from the 1740's, by the French sculptor, Cousin

ABOVE AND BELOW: *Karl XI's gallery, inspired by the Galerie des Glaces at Versailles. The decoration is of high quality, mostly by French artists. The ceiling is by Jacques Foucquet and the window embrasures are decorated by Demeaux*

suddenly changed, literally overnight, for there was now a need for an entirely new building. Already the very next day Tessin produced a plan for a grand new palace to be built on the site of the old castle. The site was a fine one – on an island in the middle of the city, with a slight eminence on which the new building could lie and dominate all around it. Unfortunately, the height of the surrounding buildings is greater now than it was in the late seventeenth century, so the palace is no longer quite such a dominant feature of the city, but in all other essentials the impressive building which we can now see standing in the centre of the beautiful city of Stockholm is the one which Tessin planned for his royal master in 1697.

Tessin had been much impressed by Italian late-renaissance and baroque buildings during his European tour, and the exterior of his new palace bears witness to this admiration, for it is in rather a severe style, obviously much influenced by such buildings as Caprarola and the Pitti Palace. This severity is relieved by pompous entrances in the south and west façades and should have been further softened by a series of statues which were to have been placed along the top of the otherwise quite uncompromising skyline. By the time the building was ready to receive these statues, however, Charles XI was dead and the dashing young Charles XII was on the throne. The new King certainly believed in the Absolute Monarchy and he liked a certain degree of splendour around him, but he was primarily a soldier and needed money for his military ventures in Russia and Poland. He considered these statues unnecessary and refused to allow Tessin to commission them, even though they were an important feature of the palace exterior. Without them, the building presents a somewhat grim appearance, especially when seen from a distance across the water. The charming mid-eighteenth-century engravings reproduced on page 248 show how it was intended to look, with statues along the parapet. In most other respects, however, Tessin had his way, and there are impressive groups of statues from this period around the entrances and in the vestibule.

The interior of the palace is quite different. Except in the chapel, where he followed the example of Bernini and Algardi, Tessin did not use an Italian style indoors but preferred to follow the latest French taste as embodied in Louis XIV's Versailles which he had so much admired.

Tessin was quite remarkably well informed about the current French tastes. He was in continual correspondence with the Swedish Ambassador in Paris who sent back detailed reports on the latest fashions in all the fields of decoration and on the artistic life of the French capital and court. Furnished with this intelligence, Tessin knew exactly where to turn when he wanted help with his many various projects. For instance, in the 1690's, he commissioned Jean Berain himself to design a state coach for the King of Sweden. This can still be seen in Stockholm, although it has been slightly altered since Tessin's day. And when he invited French artists to Sweden to help with the embellishment of the palace he engaged men well versed in the new fashions – the sculptor, Réné Chauveau, for example, a pupil of the great Girardon; Jacques Demeaux, a follower of Berain and the man who executed the faithfully Berainesque grotesques in the window embrasures of the Karl XI Gallery; and Jean-François Cousinet, the accomplished silversmith who produced the lovely silver font for the chapel which gives one an idea of the silver furniture that once stood about in the *Grands Appartements* at Versailles.

These, and a handful of other French artists, came over in the 1690's. Some of them had already been engaged for some years on a new wing to the old castle when the fire broke out. The wing itself was somehow saved and was incorporated by Tessin into his plan for the great new palace. The main structure of the new building, which is a large one, was ready and the decoration of some of the state apartments was more or less completed by about 1710 when work finally came to a standstill for lack of money. Charles XII's campaigns had cost his country dear and the Swedish state at last found itself bankrupt. The Frenchmen drifted off home and Tessin was forced to bide his time, impatiently awaiting the day when the work on his great creation could be resumed.

Work on the palace did not start again until 1728, and in that same year Nicodemus Tessin died. He had, however, brought up his son, Carl Gustav Tessin, to be as full of enthusiasm for everything French as he had been himself, and, on his death, the son took over the direction of the work on the palace. Old Tessin had also trained a young Swede named Carl Hårleman to take an important part in the great architectural enterprise and, when Tessin died, Hårleman was able to step in and organise the day-to-day work at the palace under the general supervision of Carl Gustav Tessin. Hårleman had been trained in Paris in the 1720's under that brilliant architect François-Antoine Vassé, and he paid two more visits to the French capital, in 1731 and in 1744–45, refreshing and bringing his ideas up to date each time. These close connections with France were strengthened when Carl Gustav Tessin spent several years as Swedish Ambassador to the French Court, during which period (1739–42) he steeped himself in French cultural life. He had his portrait painted by Tocque and by Aved, and his wife sat for Nattier. He was a friend of Boucher's – although this does not seem to have stopped him having an affair with Boucher's wife, who has been immortalised in the famous portrait by her husband which shows her lazing demurely on a *chaise-longue*. Tessin was quick

Part of the chapel with the pulpit by J. P. Bouchardon

Tessin's imposing south vestibule

The west staircase, part of the late seventeenth-century work, with J. P. Bouchardon's charming bronze lantern-groups of 1762

Detail of the ceiling of the White Sea Gallery. The ceiling and 'balconies' were painted by Domenico Francia in the 1730's

The Stockholm palace reflects Tessin's intimate knowledge of contemporary Parisian taste

Gustav III's Museum of Antiquities, founded in 1792

LEFT: *The Audience Chamber with its carved, and painted ceiling (1700) and Queen Christina's Coronation tapestries. The canopy (detail, above) was originally placed over Gustavus Adlophus' nuptial bed (1611–32)*

255

ABOVE AND BELOW: *Details of carved panels executed in the 1730's and 1740's respectively*

to appreciate the new neo-classical spirit in French art when it appeared, soon after 1750, and even had the main room of his own country house in Sweden decorated during the 1750's in a very advanced kind of *Louis Seize*. He admired the paintings of Chardin, which argues a certain independence of judgement and he acquired several specimens and many other fine examples of French painting more typical of their period – Bouchers, Lancrets, Oudrys, etc – and a vast number of drawings.

Between them, these two francophiles, Carl Gustav Tessin and Carl Hårleman, saw the palace all but completed, and completed virtually as old Tessin had planned it, but brought up to date in the details – most notably in the charming decoration of the less formal rooms, much of which was designed by Hårleman himself or at least under his personal supervision. With his perceptive appreciation of the contemporary French idiom, he was able to create, more than a thousand miles from Paris, interiors which are among the finest surviving monuments to the various phases of French taste during the reign of Louis XV – the firm but graceful symmetry of the Regency style, the swirling yet controlled rhythms of the early rococo, and the brilliantly balanced intricacies of the high rococo just before it stiffened and turned into *Louis Seize*. All this can be seen in room after room of the Stockholm Palace. Much has been changed since Hårleman completed his task but much still survives.

A great deal of all this rich decoration is the work of French artists brought over, as in the time of old Tessin, especially for the purpose. Since most of them spent the greater part of their working lives in Sweden, few of their names are now known outside that country, but several of them were exceptionally talented, even by the standards of an age when talent in this field was by no means rare. Particularly notable was a brother of the famous sculptor Edmé Bouchardon, Jacques-Phillippe Bouchardon who unfortunately died at quite an early age in Stockholm. He executed the superb pulpit in the chapel and the delightful bronze lanterns on the west staircase. Of the same high calibre was Charles-Guillaume Cousin, also a sculptor and a pupil of the Coustou brothers, who was responsible for much excellent work about the palace. To help out with the decorative painting, Tessin tried to persuade Lancret and Oudry to come to Stockholm, but in vain; instead he got an extremely competent pupil of Claude Audran, a man named Guillaume Taraval, who, like Boucher, had worked under Lemoine. Soon after his arrival in 1732, Taraval was engaged on the painting of the ceiling of the large room now known as the White Sea Gallery. In this fairly considerable undertaking he worked in collaboration with an Italian artist, a certain Domenico Francia who was a pupil of the well-known theatre decorator, Guiseppe Galli Bibiena. Francia and a compatriot named Ferretti, also a painter, were the only important foreign artists engaged in the original decoration of the palace who were not French.

To all this splendour, produced on the spot mainly by French artists assisted by Swedes and all under Hårleman's guidance, were now added a quantity of fine furnishings brought specially from Paris – Boucher tapestries, magnificent furniture, sumptuous silver dinner-services, Savonnerie carpets, gilt-bronze candelabra and decorative paintings. The remaining furnishings were made in Stockholm, mostly in close imitation of French originals, in Swedish workshops under the supervision of French artisans. Hårleman himself seems to have designed some furniture but, from 1745 onwards, he was able to leave this activity to yet another French-trained Swede, Jean Eric Rehn. Rehn was a brilliant draughtsman and was to design many noteworthy features in the palace. He also designed furniture, tapestries and silk-hangings for this and the other Swedish royal palaces. At first he merely elaborated schemes thought up by Hårleman but, as his experience and confidence grew, he took on increasingly important commissions, so that, when Hårleman died in 1753, Rehn was in a position to continue where his master left off, and see the palace completed.

The Swedish Royal Family finally moved into the palace in 1754. By that time almost all the rooms were finished and the last suites were being decorated by Rehn, working under a new chief architect in Hårleman's place. Rehn visited Paris in 1755–56 and brought back with him a taste for the cooler spirit of the early *Louis Seize* style with its classicising overtones. This is reflected in the rooms he decorated during the second half of the 1750's, after his return to Stockholm. In these, the rococo spirit predominates but there is a frigid elegance about much of it.

The history of the Stockholm Palace does not stop in 1760. Each successive monarch has altered some part of the great building to suit his needs or his tastes, and many of these subsequent alterations have been very successful. But the really remarkable thing about the palace is the building and the original decoration. For even though the exterior is built in an Italianate style, the plan of the building and the arrangement of the rooms was inspired directly by the Versailles of Louis XIV, while the decoration of the interior is almost entirely in the French style, so that the Stockholm Palace is in fact one of the principal monuments outside France of French art from the golden age of Louis XIV and Louis XV. The Swedes simplified the French idiom to a certain extent, largely for lack of money, but the idiom is rendered in a manner that is very much purer than that of the many other imitations of the Versailles formula found elsewhere on the continent of Europe.

PETER THORNTON

Carl Hårleman (1700–53) who designed much of the detail in the French style. He was trained in Paris in the 1720's by Francois-Antoine Vassé

Overdoor of Sofia Albertina's Audience Room. The painting is by Boucher and the frame by Rehn

Rehn's drawings for the lanterns on the staircase, sculptured by Bouchardon

A view from the centre of the 'square' with Levetzau's palace in the background

An eighteenth-century engraving of one of the palaces forming the Amalienborg Plads

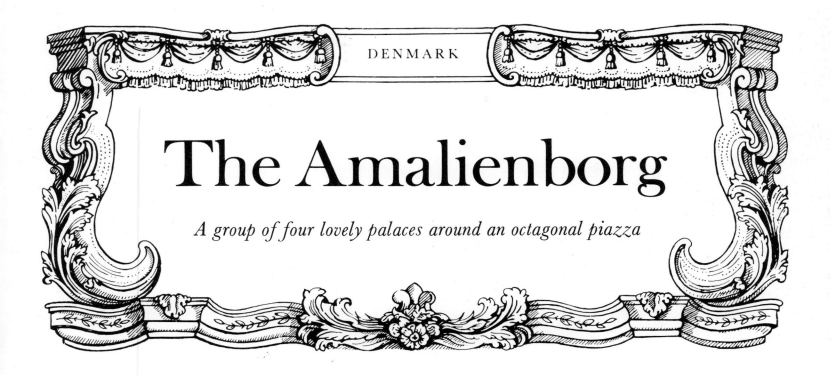

The Amalienborg

A group of four lovely palaces around an octagonal piazza

THE ROYAL RESIDENCE in Copenhagen is generally known as Amalienborg. The castle is not one great palatial structure but consists of four palaces each standing alone round an octagonal courtyard. This is the Amalienborg Plads ('Place' or 'Square'), so called after the old castle Sofie Amalienborg, which was built in 1667 by King Frederik III's queen Sofie Amalie, practically in the space occupied by the Amalienborg Plads. Sofie Amalienborg was burnt down as early as 1689. The great garden of the castle, however, did survive. At the back of the garden, and in line with it, was a military parade-ground which was rather larger than the garden. When the whole of this area was built over in the eighteenth century, in the centre of it a square was laid out which was given the name Amalienborg Plads. The square was surrounded by four separate palaces, which were built by four different noblemen for their own private use. At that period Christiansborg was the royal residence in Copenhagen. It was not until 1794, when Christiansborg was burnt down and the Royal Family were rendered homeless, that the then King, Christian VII, bought three of the palaces on Amalienborg Plads, while one of them had already come into royal ownership and had been used for a military academy. Since 1794 all the four palaces have belonged to the Danish kings and have been regarded as one castle known as Amalienborg. This development is the result of a successful enterprise in town architecture of which Danish people are proud.

It all began in 1749, when Frederik V, probably on the prompting of some of his ministers, contemplated the development of

Jacques Saly's equestrian statue of Frederik V, presented to him by the Asiatic Company, was erected in the Amalienborg Plads in 1768

259

the area already mentioned. The idea was to commemorate in this way the 300th anniversary of the Oldenborg royal house. Frederik V came of Oldenborg stock and the new quarter was to bear the name Frederiksstaden.

During the autumn of 1749 the final plans for development were elaborated by the royal architect, Nicolai Eigtved. The original idea was to divide the rectangular area into four equal parts by means of two intersecting streets. Exactly in the middle, where the streets met, there was to be a large square. The final plan did retain the placing of the two streets – Amaliegade and Frederiksgade, as they are always called – but from the area in the direction of the harbour half was sliced off, so that if a fire should occur it would not endanger the fleet anchored there. In addition, the large square was now made octagonal, and facing the western end of Frederiksgade another plot was included, where a large, imposing church – Frederikskirken – was to be built. The plan also included an up-to-date hospital – Frederiks Hospital – at the northern end of the area, west of Amaliegade. Apart from the sites around Amalienborg Plads the whole space was handed over to the corporation of Copenhagen, which was

An aerial view of Copenhagen showing the Amalienborg Plads in the centre

An eighteenth-century engraving by Le Clerc of the 'square' with Frederik's Marble Church behind

OPPOSITE: *The north-western palace on the Amalienborg, originally built for Count von Levetzau*

261

The Riddersalen, decorated with richly carved boiseries in the German rococo style

thereafter to have control over the sale of sites. To ensure homogeneity in the development of that large area it was stipulated, among other things, that the windows of the various houses should be on the same level. Furthermore, designs for houses were to be approved by the King before they were put into execution. In April 1750 the first citizens came forward with building projects. As these proved unsatisfactory, the King decided on April 28 that all owners of a house being built should report to Eigtved, who would supply designs free of charge.

This plan could not after all be carried out completely. For one thing, Eigtved died in 1754, and for another, just at this time a considerable change in the style of architecture was taking place, as we know, all over Europe, rococo being ousted increasingly by the neo-classic style. But all the same, Frederiksstaden became an exceptionally homogeneous quarter in Copenhagen, and in spite of many later demolitions, and in particular the disrespect of more recent times, Frederiksstaden can still be

One of the guest bedrooms at Amalienborg, used by Queen Elizabeth II during her State Visit to Denmark

considered one of the most beautiful parts of the Danish capital.

As regards Amalienborg Plads, of course very special care was bestowed on its buildings. Probably the fact that the 'place' became octagonal instead of square as originally planned was due to the German architect Marcus Tuscher, who was trained in Italy. In any case he was responsible for the tripartite form of each palace, which consisted of one main structure combined with two lower pavilions flanking it. Eigtved had first proposed an identical height of cornice all round the 'place', so that it would have been given a uniform character rather like, for instance, Place Vendôme in Paris. Tuscher's tripartite system with a baroque stamp was preferred, and Eigtved had to alter his drawings accordingly, though in such a way that his proposed division of the central part with high double pillars and pilasters, as also his façade style on the whole, remained unaltered. The result was thus a compromise, such as occurred at about the same time in Paris in the competition for the present Place de la

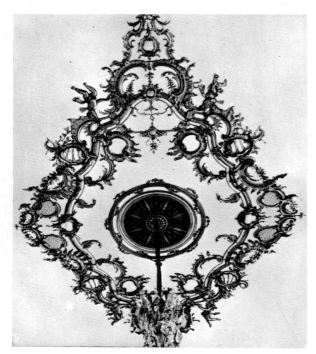

A detail of the stucco ceiling in the Riddersalen by J. B. Fossati

A detail of the fountain in the dining-room. The vase is modelled after a design by Jacques Saly

Concorde. Acquaintance with the Paris competition, moreover, may well have had a certain significance for the creation of Amalienborg Plads. There are also striking points of similarity in principle between this and Mansart's much older plan and development of the present Place Hoche in Versailles.

It was not until after the final front elevation for the palaces was ready that the sites were presented by the King in 1750 to four noblemen, but on the condition that the façades of the palaces should correspond exactly to Eigtved's design, while the gentlemen were left free with regard to the interior. The four chosen persons were: Geheimeraad Joachim von Brockdorff, General Greve C. F. von Levetzau, Baron Severin Leopold Løvenskiold and Overhofmarskal Greve Adam Gottlob Moltke.

A. G. Moltke was the one among these four best qualified in every way as the owner of a house in building. Besides being very rich, he was one of the King's closest friends and, in addition, unquestionably one of the most influential men in the country. He was, moreover, a man of wide culture and is rightly regarded as having been one of Denmark's greatest personalities in the eighteenth century. His interest in art of every kind was intense, and he was actively engaged in the encouragement of art, for instance in his office of President of the Academy of Art. It is therefore easy to understand that such a man would do his utmost to make his winter abode in Copenhagen a model of an aristocratic residence. Moltke's palace in Amalienborg Plads became, indeed, incomparably the most magnificent private residence in the country. The history of the creation of the palace is known in detail, thanks to the thorough research done by the Danish scholars Mario Krohn and Chr. Elling.

In August 1750 the foundations of Moltke's palace were already finished, and in the following summer the first storey was completed and the next storey begun. In March 1754 the palace was occupied for the first time. Three months later the architect Eigtved died. Although at this moment not everything in the interior was finished, Eigtved managed to supervise and to set the seal of his artistry on the whole of Moltke's palace, apart from the dining-hall, which will be discussed afterwards.

Whereas the façade has been influenced by German rococo architecture, the distribution of rooms in the palace is altogether in keeping with the principles that had formed the basis of French civil architecture in the first half of the eighteenth century. It is also in keeping with French practice that the decoration of the rooms observed a certain etiquette. The entrance hall, for example, where the back wall was concave, from its classical pillars in blue-grey Norwegian marble acquired a more severe and imposing character than the large salon, where the rich, gilt rocaille decorations struck a gay and festive note.

This large salon, *Riddersalen* (the Baronial Hall) as it is now called, is one of the two most magnificent rooms in the palace. Even by comparison with the best rococo halls it occupies a position of dignity in the hierarchy. The white panelled walls, like the doors, are embellished with richly carved and gilt ornaments. Exuberance is curbed by an almost rhythmical division of the space. Doors, windows and mirrors and two large fireplaces provide for that. In relation to corresponding French rooms the size and decoration of the hall, even so, are rather exaggerated. In particular, such heavy stucco decorations in the ceiling would not have found favour in Paris. The style of the Riddersalen is derived in large measure from German decorative style at that period. There are thus distinct points of similarity with decorative engravings by Francois de Cuvilliés, an artist active in Munich, by whom Eigtved had formerly been employed.

The stucco ceiling was the work of the Italian J. B. Fossati, the wood carvings were by the Frenchman Louis-Auguste Le Clerc. The life-size portraits, representing King Frederik V and Queen Juliane Marie, were painted by Louis Tocqué, while the pictures above the fireplaces and doors are by François Boucher. Also, in another room in the palace, there is a series of tapestries from cartoons by Boucher, which were woven in Beauvais.

One of the rooms that Eigtved did not live to achieve was the dining-hall beside the Riddersalen. It was carried out in the neo-classic style by the Frenchman Nicolas-Henri Jardin, who had come to Copenhagen in 1755, called in to submit a design for the proposed Frederikskirke. The dining-hall was begun and completed in 1757 and thus, with its free-standing, classical pillars, is a very early example of the reaction towards rococo. For the history of Danish architecture it would be gratifying if this piece of modern decoration could be dated as earlier than any French example. But there is no certainty of that. At all events more light will have to be thrown on the history of Parisian interior decoration in these critical years, especially as regards the interiors of the Palais Royal, before the dining-hall is pronounced number one in the line.

King Christian VII took over Moltke's palace in 1794 and made it his residence. On that occasion some alterations to the interior were carried out under the direction of the architect C. F. Harsdorff. In addition, the low connecting portions between the main building and the pavilions were raised by one storey, and this was done also in the other three palaces. At the same time a colonnade in the Ionic style was erected as a link between Christian VII's palace and the earlier Løvenskiold's palace where the Crown Prince had now moved in.

The present King and Queen of Denmark live in the earlier Brockdorff palace, which only differs from the others externally in its possession of a clock high up on the façade.

SVEND ERIKSEN

A ground-plan of the complex of palaces in the eighteenth century

Kronborg

Hamlet's pinnacled castle at Elsinore on the Baltic shore

The south-east tower. The original castle, erected by King Erik of Pomerania in the fifteenth century, was later incorporated in the present castle

OPPOSITE: *The west wing of Kronborg. The King's Tower is in the left foreground and the spire of the Trumpeter's Tower rises in the centre*

KRONBORG IS SITUATED outside Elsinore, on the coast, forty kilometres north of Copenhagen, and on the promontory farthest to the north-east of Zealand. Although close to Elsinore, Kronborg is not really, and never has been, that town's citadel. Even more than is the case today, Kronborg in former times stood apart from Elsinore. In those days, as the old pictures show, the open stretch between the castle and the town was still broader, and the great fortifications then as now surrounded the castle only, while the town remained defenceless.

Kronborg stands at the narrowest part of the Sound between Denmark and Sweden. On the journey by sea from the north towards Copenhagen the towers of the castle are the first thing to come into view. In former times this sight certainly more often than not gave cause for mixed feelings, especially to captains of foreign merchant vessels. For, from 1425 until 1857, the ships had to cast anchor at Kronborg and there pay a toll for passage through the Sound, both sides of which until 1660 were Danish territory. As this toll yielded a large revenue, which went direct to the King's own privy purse, the Danish kings bestowed great care on Kronborg, which by virtue of its guns was expected to ensure payment of the toll.

It was in the reign of King Erik of Pomerania that the Sound Dues were introduced, and he was the founder of the first castle near Elsinore. Its name was Krogen (the Hook), taken from the hook-like point on which it was built. Krogen, so far as modern excavations have shown, was very primitive and in its architecture entirely medieval in character. The castle consisted of a

KRONBORG

OPPOSITE

ABOVE: *An angle of the fortress, dominated by the Trumpeter's Tower (left) which was originally built by Steenwinckel after the fire of 1629, and rebuilt by Harsdorff in 1777 after it had been struck by lightning. The tower acquired its name because from it the King's heralds blew signals across land and sea*

BELOW: *Kronborg stands in a strategic position at the tip of a promontory on the narrowest part of the Sound between Denmark and Sweden. Since the days of Christian IV, Kronborg has not been the home of royalty, but has been used as a fortress, a garrison and a prison and is now a museum*

RIGHT: *The fortification seen from the south after an engraving by Samuel Pufendorf, c. 1696. The view shows the additional fortifications constructed on the landward side in the reign of Christian V, 1670–99*

The north-west corner of the courtyard with the King's Tower in the background. The style is northern renaissance, with echoes of the Netherlands.

strong wall surrounding an almost square courtyard with various buildings placed in the corners and along the walls. The remains of that castle are preserved in the present Kronborg, in particular a hall with wooden pillars and frescos in the north wing of the castle and a banqueting-hall with vaulting in the west wing.

As early as 1558–59 King Christian III began to modernise the old castle. This, however, was chiefly a matter of the defensive works which, after the appearance of more powerful cannon, were behind the times. In 1574 his son, King Frederik II, undertook new extensions and improvements of both the castle itself and its defences. The north and west wing of the castle was reconstructed and the conversion of the south wing into a church was begun. The architect was Hans van Paeschen, who was probably of Flemish extraction and had previously been at work in Sweden. The materials for the rebuilding were red bricks alternating with horizontal bands of sandstone. The window-frames were also of sandstone, while the roof was of red tiles. The interior and exterior of the magnificent main entrance to the present castle date from this period of building, as does also the so-called *Mørkeport* (dark gate). Over this gateway there is an inscription in German which tells how in 1577 Frederik built the castle and called it Kronborg. On January 24, 1577 the King issued an open letter announcing that Krogen in future was to be called Kronborg. Breaches of this rule would mean the forfeit of a good ox.

It is not altogether clear what this first Kronborg looked like. Very probably, after all, the reconstruction was rather bungled and the result must have been a jumble of old and new. It is likely that the maximum effort was devoted to modernising

the encircling ramparts with strong defensive bastions.

At all events, Frederik II already during the year 1577 decided to carry out a fresh extension and complete reconstruction of Kronborg, this time on a much more definite and original plan. On June 30, 1577 Hans van Paeschen's successor was appointed in the person of the Flemish architect and fortification works engineer, Anthonis van Opbergen, who was born in Malines in 1543, one of a well-known family of artists.

In 1585 the new Kronborg was practically finished. It now consisted of four connected wings three storeys high, all the walls faced with grey sandstone. The roof tiling had been replaced by copper. Round the windows and on the many gables there was a profusion of decorative sculptures, and above the roofs rose copper-clad towers and spires. In the centre of the castle courtyard a great octagonal fountain with bronze figures had been erected, cast in Nuremberg by Georg Labenwolf. The interior of the castle also was adorned with rich furnishings. Among these were forty tapestries, woven in Elsinore 1581–89, after designs by the Flemish painter Hans Knieper. The tapestries represented one hundred kings who had reigned before Frederik II, also Frederik II and his son, the future Christian IV. Many of the kings depicted were legendary kings mentioned by the historian, Saxo. With the tapestries there was a magnificent canopy.

The distinctly military purpose of Kronborg, already mentioned, is undoubtedly the reason why Kronborg in its architecture is so different from other more or less contemporary Danish buildings, whose style, like Kronborg's, must be characterised by the very broad term 'Scandinavian renaissance style'. This, at least where Denmark is concerned, is a style in which decoration plays far the most important part, whereas the plan is still rather medieval, despite certain efforts to pay attention to symmetry. The decoration has generally been inspired by, if not directly copied from, Flemish and German copperplate engravings, and besides, many of the stone-masons working in Denmark at the time had been brought from the Netherlands. The individual parts of the decoration had been fashioned chiefly on models from ancient or renaissance Italy. That age could, therefore, with a certain justification, call the style 'renaissance', though with the addition of 'Scandinavian'. Through the decoration the buildings could be clad in a garb that answered their purpose. A royal hunting-lodge like Frederiksborg, where considerations of defence are kept as unobtrusive as possible, is decorated in a light, gay and festive style. If the decorative style of this castle is compared with the prints in the illustrated textbooks of the period, such as those by Vredeman de Vries, the undoubted conclusion must be that its classification is either Ionic or Corinthian. Kronborg's decorations, on the other hand, are comparatively heavy, severe and solemn in

The Queen's Chamber with ceiling paintings by Morten van Steenwinckel (1596–1646)

The Gallery in the east wing, with seventeenth-century Dutch furniture

OPPOSITE

ABOVE: *The King's Chamber, which was restored after the fire of 1629*
BELOW: *The Great Hall, 200 by 36 feet, is said to be the largest hall in Northern Europe. It is also known as the Knight's Hall*

An alcove with ceiling decoration, illustrating the coolness and simplicity characteristic of the interior architecture of Kronborg

A view into one of the rooms in the north wing which contains Danish chairs from the early eighteenth century

style, with a rugged, imposing effect like that of a splendid suit of armour. Anyone with some knowledge of architecture at that time would certainly, without hesitation, call the style of Kronborg either Tuscan or Doric.

The royal castle aspect of Kronborg is accentuated externally by the richness of the ornamentation, by the numerous large windows and the many decorated gables and spires. In addition, the magnificence of the castle is thrown into relief by the massive fortifications, which today, after all, are considerably more extensive than they were originally.

In the night between September 24 and 25, 1629, Kronborg was ravaged by a terrible fire, which left nothing but the walls, apart from a few tower rooms and in particular the church, which is still seen in its original form and with its old furnishings. King Christian IV, in 1631, began the rebuilding of Kronborg, this being carried out in defiance of the *Rigsraad* (Imperial Council), whose opinion was that in view of the country's undeniably serious financial situation they could not agree to it. Christian IV replied by taking the money from the Sound Dues fund, of which he had complete control. In addition the Sound Dues were doubled for some time.

The chief architect for the rebuilding was Hans van Steenwinckel the Younger, whose father had been one of the Flemish master builders called in to Kronborg in 1578. Undoubtedly Christian IV wished to re-create the work of his father, Frederik II. Christian IV is the one of all Danish kings who knew most about art. He had a special interest in architecture, and some of Denmark's finest buildings date from his reign. Some scholars even think that Christian IV was a competent architect. At all events, he enjoyed drawing.

Of the alterations that were carried out under Christian IV, almost all arose from practical considerations. The most obvious change must have been that the great tower of Kronborg was deprived of its domed top, which had previously served as a belfry. In addition, the small gables were set flush with the walls, at the same time being heightened. This must have given the castle façade a rather more subdued appearance than before. But apart from these variations Kronborg, externally, is on the whole just as it was in Frederik II's time.

During the wars with Sweden in the seventeenth century, after a three weeks' siege in 1658, Kronborg was captured by the Swedes. The castle suffered grievously during the wars and in 1659 it was sacked. The Swedes carried off, among other things, the figures from the fountain in the castle courtyard and many paintings, as well as the canopy previously mentioned, which is now in the Stockholm National Museum. Fourteen of the tapestries belonging to it have been preserved, while the rest went up in flames in the fire at Frederiksborg Castle in 1859.

A rusticated doorway of the Palace of Kronborg

BELOW: *A detail of the chapel which was conse-crated in 1582. While most of the furniture of the castle was destroyed in the fire of 1629, the chapel was spared, and the original oak furnishings, vividly coloured and gilded, have been preserved*

In the reign of King Christian V a new outer fortification was constructed on the landward side, and in 1690 the outer gateway, with rich baroque decorations, was erected. It is the first of the gateways to be passed on entry into Kronborg today. In the eighteenth century certain alterations were undertaken, for instance the largest tower, which was burnt when struck by lightning in 1774, was re-erected in the original style.

Whereas Kronborg had formerly been reserved for the King's use, in 1785 it was requisitioned as an ordinary military barracks, and the castle functioned as such until 1922. After its use by the military, during which more especially the interior of the castle had been badly damaged and altered beyond recognition with, for example, additional floors, partition walls etc., inserted, a thorough restoration was carried out. It was then decided that the King's and Queen's rooms on the main floor – the third floor – of the castle, together with smaller rooms adjacent, should be refurnished in such a way that they might give an idea of the royal splendour which had once reigned in the castle. With this object in view many valuable pieces of furniture, paintings and tapestries have been acquired, which in their style and quality may be regarded as suited to the castle, and which on a sound historical basis impart a sense of real occupation to the rooms. Guidance for this was obtained from a few old lists of furniture from Kronborg and other northern European castles of the same period, as well as contemporary paintings of interiors. Kronborg now belongs to the Danish State, but to a great extent these expenses have been defrayed by the Carlsberg Foundation.

SVEND ERIKSEN

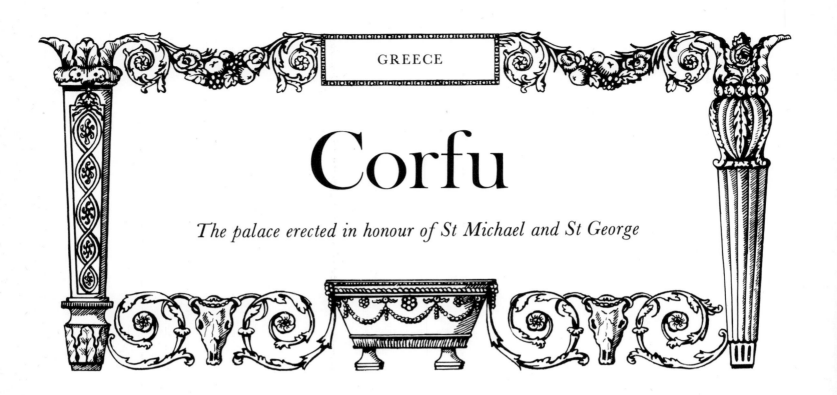

Corfu

The palace erected in honour of St Michael and St George

The Doric colonnade that runs the length of the façade and shelters the entrance from the sun

OPPOSITE: *The palace dates from 1819, during the British occupation of Corfu. Originally the figure of Britannia surmounted the central pediment*

THE VISITOR TO CORFU who wishes to see the palace, is invariably asked, 'Which palace?' For this incomparably beautiful island, pricked with cypresses and cacti and serrated round the edges by a gently gnawing sea, contains three of them. There is the Achilleion, the villa built by the tragic Empress Elizabeth of Austria in 1890, and subsequently bought by Kaiser Wilhelm II; *Mon Repos*, originally the private residence of the British High Commissioner and now the summer villa of the Greek Royal Family; and the Royal Palace in the centre of the town, known to cultured Corfiots as the Palace of St Michael and St George. It is the latter which is described in these pages.

The palace acquired this unexpected name by the coincidence that the Ionian islands passed under British protection in 1815 shortly before the Prince Regent founded the Order of St Michael and St George, an honour which was originally confined to those who had served His Majesty in the Mediterranean, but is now awarded for exceptional merit in any part of the Foreign Service. The Order needed a focal point at the same moment as the first British High Commissioner of the Ionian islands demanded a suitable building in Corfu for ceremonial occasions, and a chamber for the legislature of the Heptanese.

All three functions are apparent in the architecture and decoration of the palace, the foundation stone of which was laid on St George's Day, 1819. The two great archways which flank the main façade are labelled respectively, in Greek, the Gate of the Archangel Michael and the Gate of St George. The Senate Room contains, besides a scowling bust of Sir Thomas Maitland,

CORFU

The double-headed Venetian citadel at Corfu in the late eighteenth century, before the Palace of St Michael and St George was built. The palace occupies a site just beyond the fortifications in the right foreground, from where it was overlooked by the old fortresses, among which the English constructed barracks for their soldiers

The Strada Reale ('the Royal Street') in Corfu, drawn by one of the officers of the British garrison, Lieutenant H. E. Allen, in 1832. The Italianate architecture of many of the buildings (due to the long Venetian occupation) contrasts with the Greek dress of the people

the first High Commissioner, portraits of successive Presidents of the Senate wearing across their unmistakably Hellenic chests the blue and red sash of the KCMG. The Throne Room is hung with an excellent copy of Sir Thomas Lawrence's portrait of George IV (one leg slashed by a bayonet, but dutifully repaired) and its ceiling is picked out with the emblems of the Order.

During the twenty years of Napoleon's rise and fall, the Corfiots had found themselves governed in turn by no less than five nations – the Venetians, the French (twice), the Turks, the Russians and finally the English. Apart from establishing there the headquarters of St George, the latest rulers of Corfu showed unexpected tact by adopting for an important feature of the new building a style derived from the Greeks, and by siting it on a piece of ground that hitherto had been no-man's-land between the old town and the Venetian citadel. It was an ideal choice, for the site was both convenient and historic, and prominent without being offensive. Today one approaches the palace along the length of the Esplanade – a name suggestive of Bournemouth,

The upper hall of the palace. Colonel Whitmore, the architect, was an officer in the Royal Engineers. He wrote: 'I was forced to model almost every particle of the building, and I think there were no less than eight or nine different languages spoken by the workmen'

but in fact a vast open space on which Venetian soldiers once exercised and today Corfiot boys, proudly unique among non-Commonwealth youth, play cricket.

At the far end, with its back to the sea, rises a dignified Regency mansion. One would not immediately sense in it a palace; rather, one would say, a club in Pall Mall, or a noble-man's house in southern Ireland. Yet it has its flourishes, more aristocratic than regal, in the long Doric portico which extends beyond the whole width of the façade into a curved porch on either side, and in the two archways which add to the Regency-Greek stoa a touch of Rome. That on the left is now a roadway leading to the harbour; that on the right is closed by a low wall which overlooks the garden twenty feet below. Both owe much to the sunlight with which the building is bathed from different angles throughout the day, and which gives the stone, imported at heavy cost from Malta, a golden creaminess that compensates for the flaking and discoloration which it has suffered during the 150 rainy winters and scorching summers since it was cut.

277

The main staircase, leading to the upper hall, with a particularly fine wrought-iron balustrade

The lower, or entrance, hall, beautifully restored by Jean Collas in the period after World War II

OPPOSITE: *The circular hall, which divides the Throne Room from the State Dining-room, is considered the most beautiful room in the palace*

Seen from the rear, there is no trace of ostentation, and everything but simple elegance has been eliminated from the little courtyard enclosed by the two projecting wings. It was not the view landwards from the harbour that concerned the architect, but the view outwards from the windows of the first floor over the little island of Vido to the mountainous mainland coast ten miles beyond, where Greece divides from Albania. Here again, one is struck by the absence of any proconsular display. The palace was a compromise between the attractive and the splendid, a building that was frankly British and saw no need to compete with the vast Venetian engineering of the citadel on the one side nor the balconied French façades on the other. Of all European palaces, this must be the least aloof from its immediate surroundings and the most tactful in its suggestion of suzerainty.

It comes therefore as a surprise to learn that the architect was a British soldier. Colonel (afterwards General Sir George) Whitmore was an officer in the Royal Engineers, attached to the Corfu garrison for the purpose. In his unpublished memoirs, recently unearthed by Mr Stelio Hourmouzios, Whitmore described the difficulties by which he was beset. It was only after his design had been approved that he was told that the legislative chamber was to be housed under the same roof; and the parsimony which hampered his first designs was gradually relaxed as the work progressed (a strange experience for an architect) and he was obliged to spend on the embellishment of the interior what he would have gladly earmarked at an earlier stage on the design as a whole.

His success as master craftsman can be appreciated by close study of the detail of exterior and interior. The triglyph frieze and *guttae* above the frontal portico, and the cornices of the high wings at the back, prepare the visitor for the Adam-like care with which the ornamentation of the main rooms was executed. Leading directly from the paved floor of the colonnade, without any intervening step, one enters a hall, an *atrium* that extends the whole depth of the building to a noble flight of stairs at its far end. On either side is a peristyle composed of fourteen Ionic columns mounted on a stylobate four steps high. The curtain walls are broken by great mahogany doors, reminiscent of those at Claydon House in Buckinghamshire, leading to the Senate Room and other offices. This hall has great coolness in contrast to the glare outside, an impression derived from its relative darkness and silence, almost as if one found oneself in the anteroom to a Roman bath.

By the grand staircase beyond, with its high central window and exquisite metal balustrade, one mounts to the principal floor, which is divided into the three main reception rooms – a circular hall or rotunda in the centre, leading to two large rooms of equal dimensions, the Throne Room on the left and the State

Dining-room on the right. Of these the rotunda is the most successful. Its domed roof is set with plaques of wedgwood blue and classical statues stand in niches around the walls. They are further pierced equidistantly by three doors and a window, and a beautiful crystal chandelier completes the perfect proportion. The Throne Room would be more acceptable without the throne (which in the absence of true royalty must have seemed faintly ridiculous even in 1820), and the children's-corner painting of St George attacking a *papier-mâché* dragon. St Michael, a copy from a Guido Reni, is less offensive. Its best feature, however, is a musicians' gallery high above the door, with a bow-fronted grill constructed with such delicacy that one would fear for the fate of any musicians mounted upon it, even musicians with the slender physique of the average Corfiot.

When the Ionian islands were ceded to Greece in 1864, the palace served as a royal residence until the Second World War, having miraculously survived Mussolini's bombardment of the town in reprisal for the Janina murders. It suffered greater damage from its use as a temporary billet for the refugees from Epirus during the Greek civil war. The interior was left in so dilapidated a condition that the Greek state was only able to restore part of it, and a private trust organised by Sir Charles Peake, then British Ambassador in Athens, undertook in 1954 to pay for the restoration of the three state rooms on the first floor, 'as a memorial to the British connection with Greece and as a notable example of the English architectural style of the period'. The work was admirably executed under the direction of the gifted Corfiot architect, Jean Collas, who restored with only minor modifications the decorative scheme when it was known, and improvised from his knowledge of the Regency style when it was not. The King of Greece still occasionally uses the palace on state occasions while in residence at his nearby villa, *Mon Repos*, and several of the former British High Commissioner's private apartments now house the archaeological treasures recovered by the excavations at Corcyra, the celebrated Corinthian colony that lay a mile south of the modern town.

The palace of St Michael and St George is included in this book not because it is a 'great' palace in the formal sense, but because its unusual origins and associations, and the manner in which it blends a very English tradition with a true respect for things Greek, give it exceptional interest for the student both of architecture and of political history. There it stands, faintly mottled by time and tribulation, grey or glowing according to the disposition of the weather, but as much loved by the Corfiots and their King as if it had been erected for Greeks by Greeks, instead of by a frustrated Colonel of Engineers for the rather surly representative of a foreign power.

NIGEL NICOLSON

A view of the throne from the door of one of the two largest rooms in the palace. The ceiling is picked out with the emblems of the Order. Contemporary accounts reveal that the High Commissioner did not seat himself on the throne but stood on the step beside it

OPPOSITE: *The Throne Room, with the paintings of St George and of St Michael on either side of a portrait of George IV, a copy of Sir Thomas Lawrence's original. This was the symbolic headquarters of the Order of St Michael and St George until 1864*

The royal castle of Wawel, seen on its dominant crag from the north side overlooking the Vistula, painted by J. N. Glowacki, c. 1835

The castle and the cathedral today, viewed from the sharp bend of the river. Both castle and cathedral date from the fourteenth century

The Wawel Castle
CRACOW

The centre of a splendid historical and cultural tradition

THE VISTULA, THE MAIN ARTERY OF POLAND, has two moments of glory in its long meandering course, when it flows through the country's two capitals: through Cracow, the old capital, and then, flowing on northward in a great curve, through Warsaw, the present-day capital, two hundred miles away as the crow flies. In Cracow, the waters of the Vistula move slowly past the foot of the Wawel, the great rocky hill that overlooks the city and surrounding countryside, and from which rise the majestic walls of the fortifications, the proud outline of the cathedral with its soaring bell-tower and the massive form, lightened by its large windows, of the royal castle, where the kings of Poland used to live.

Cracovia totius Poloniae urbs celeberrima ('Cracow the most famous city of all Poland') was the description of a chronicler. And it is still true, for the old capital has had an eventful history, in which the Wawel castle has frequently had a vital part to play. As a fortified hill, the Wawel itself had occupied a position of the first importance from the very earliest times. Towards the end of the first millenium, during the formation of the Polish state (whose first capital was not, however, Cracow), the dwelling-place of the local prince was built on the Wawel, first in wood and later, during the tenth and eleventh centuries, in masonry. After 966, the official date of Poland's birth, a chapel was built there, the pre-romanesque rotunda of Our Lady (later of Saints Felix and Adauctus) which is, essentially, still in existence. Towards the middle of the fourteenth century, when Cracow had already become capital of Poland, Casimir the

The Wawel cathedral. The castle and the cathedral are part of one architectural unit, and are actually joined together on one side

283

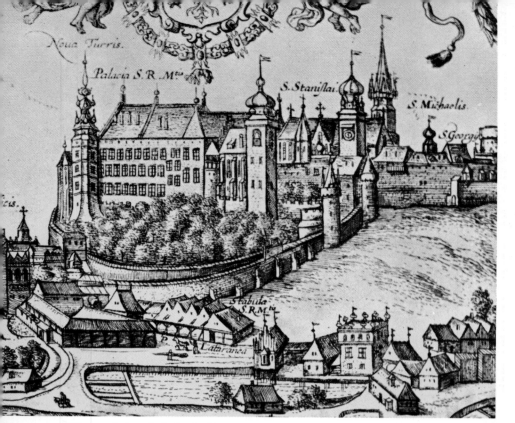

The castle in 1618, by G. Braun and F. Hogenberg, from Cosmographia

The three-storeyed arcades around the courtyard

Great had a grander, gothic palace built beside the little old one, with an inner courtyard; several towers and interiors of that period are still in existence, though considerably altered, and have been incorporated into the renaissance castle. Also during the fourteenth century a huge gothic cathedral was built beside the castle on the site of the earlier romanesque buildings; this original cathedral still stands, and contains the numerous beautiful chapels, altars, altarpieces and tombs that were added during the centuries that followed.

In 1499 most of the gothic royal palace was destroyed by fire. Naturally, since this was the height of Poland's power, it had to be rebuilt on a still grander and richer scale. Here the young prince and heir Sigismund Jagiello (who became king in 1506) intervened with his own personal taste and preferences. He was a cultured man and a patron of the arts. He had spent several years in Buda, at the court of his brother Wladyslaw, king of Hungary and Bohemia, where, towards the middle of the fifteenth century, a group of Florentines had kindled a general enthusiasm for Italian renaissance art. It was decided that the castle should be rebuilt in the new style which, at that time, had hardly penetrated beyond the borders of Italy. So a group of Florentines was sent for from Hungary and their leader, the architect and sculptor Francesco da Firenze, was put in charge of the rebuilding of the royal palace. Work began on this in 1506.

The architect appears to have respected the remaining walls of the old building; their construction did not follow the normal Italian pattern and therefore the *piano nobile* was on the second floor, not on the first as in Florentine or Roman palaces. But Francesco was mainly concerned with the exterior. To begin

Cracow in 1493, by Hartmann Schedel

The city and the palace in the fifteenth century

The Hungarian architect Berrecci built the loggia at the far end of the wing

with, for instance, he decorated the surrounds of two windows in the west wing in the pure style of the Florentine renaissance, and built an overhanging loggia there in the same style. These were perfect, but minor, examples of the influence of the *quattrocento* tradition. Francesco's main contribution, and that which gave the castle its very definite character and made it one of the most important examples of Italian renaissance architecture in the whole of Europe, was a series of three-storeyed arcades along the walls facing on to the courtyard. He died in 1516 before the work was finished, but it was continued by his successor as head of the team of Italian architects – the architect and sculptor Bartolommeo Berrecci, who had probably come from Hungary like Francesco. During the years 1517–34 he built loggias in the outer walls of each wing (though only partially on the west wing), completed those round the courtyard and directed the architectural work of the interior.

In this way the great courtyard took on the architectural shape it still has today. The calm and measured alternation of light and shade gives the majestic arches a rhythm and harmony. The yellowish sandstone emphasises the protruding parts, the columns with their Ionic capitals and the entablature – as they alternate with the openings of the arches shaded by the wide open corridors of the loggias that run along the walls of the courtyard on all floors.

Berrecci, Francesco's successor, was an extremely gifted architect, and was commissioned by King Sigismund to build a commemorative chapel next to the cathedral. This chapel, built between 1517 and 1533, is the finest work by Italians outside Italy itself. Simultaneously, Berrecci was not only supervising

285

The Tournament Room has a sixteenth-century frieze, and the 'Story of Noah' in tapestry

The wooden ceiling of the Ambassador's Hall with thirty boldly carved heads by the sculptor Sebastian Taverbach in the coffering

the building of the castle loggias but was also actively directing all the work in progress. Surrounds of several dozen doors and windows, both inside and out, were made in his workshop, and are extremely original and finely executed; the gothic motifs of the local stone-cutters intermingled with the purely renaissance ornament, and the result was a series of architectural decorations whose rhythm and unity bore the imprint of Berrecci's modern Italian spirit.

The interiors, too, were designed at the same time, but subsequent restorations and alterations, as well as war damage throughout the ages, have completely changed the original appearance of the great halls and chambers, including the grandest of all, on the second floor. The wooden beams supporting the ceiling were put up during a recent series of restorations. The Ambassadors' Hall, however, still has its original décor of carved wood: thirty boldly carved heads, worked with an exaggerated late-gothic realism by the sculptor Sebastian Tauerbach, are placed in the coffering of the ceiling. Were they members of the court, or allegorical portraits, or both? Their position in the coffering is extremely unusual, and gives the Ambassadors' Hall a very marked individuality. This room, and several others, still have the original painted friezes, though partially restored: paintings of tournaments, battle scenes and allegorical subjects, partly the work of Hans Dürer, brother of Albrecht, and of Anthony of Wroclaw. The non-religious spirit of the new age is revealed in all these paintings.

The courtyard of the Wawel Castle is a magnificent example of Italian renaissance art. The majestic placing of one set of arches above the other is reminiscent of the palaces of Florence and Pienza in particular. Yet the courtyard had one local architectural feature unknown in Italy: the columns of the upper floor, which was to all intents and purposes the *piano nobile*, are taller than they ever are in Italy, and the architect felt the need to counter the soaring upward movement by means of an encircling band of stone: the capitals support the high overhanging roof, of the kind indispensable in a northern climate though not in Italy. The survival of gothic forms, stronger in Poland than in the native country of the castle's architects, was evident in the doorways and particularly in the interiors, with their carved and painted decoration. The general impression given by the Wawel castle is that its design was inspired by Italians but, at the same time, that this design was executed in a country far removed from Italy, a country with its own artistic tradition, a cultural centre in its own right.

In the renaissance, the walls of the rooms were hung with tapestries. The son of Sigismund I, Sigismund II Augustus (1548–72), commissioned a collection of 350 tapestries from the famous workshops of the Netherlands, based partly on original

designs by Michael Coxcien, the 'Raphael of Flanders'. This collection, reduced as time passed to 150 items (in fact the finest of the originals), after a chequered career and having spent the war years in Canada, is now once again on the walls of the castle. It is a magnificent collection, one of the largest and finest in the world: there are large tapestries of biblical and mythological subjects, *pugnae ferarum* (fighting animals) and heraldic motifs. The main figures stand out against a sweeping landscape, surrounded by ornamental borders of fruit and foliage.

From the moment when the capital was transferred to Warsaw, at the end of the sixteenth century, the Wawel ceased to occupy the important position of first castle in the land. It was, however, still used by the kings when they stayed in Cracow, where the coronation continued to be held. Several interiors were redecorated in the baroque and later in the neo-classical style, thus adding variety to the predominantly renaissance interiors.

The castle, then, is an integral part of a great historical and artistic unit which grew up on the Wawel gradually, over a period of a thousand years. With its charming position, its art treasures and its historic memories, it is one of the most fascinating of all European castles.

STEFAN KOZAKIEWICZ

The Senator's Hall with some of the outstanding tapestries woven in the Netherlands in the sixteenth century

287

A note on the photographs

The authors and publishers are grateful to the present owners of the palaces illustrated in this book for permission to describe and illustrate them.

The following photographers took the photographs of the palaces mentioned against their names:

IAN GRAHAM: Hampton Court; Windsor Castle; Holyroodhouse; Versailles; Malmaison; Fontainebleau; the Royal Palace, Monaco; Huis ten Bosch; Tullgarn; the Royal Palace, Stockholm; Amalienborg; Kronborg

EDWIN SMITH: Sans Souci; the Quirinal; the Royal Palace, Naples; Caserta; the Royal Palace, Turin; Corfu

KERRY DUNDAS: Charlottenburg; Linderhof; the Alhambra; Aranjuez; the Escorial; Sintra; Queluz

FOTO LUCCA CHMEL, VIENNA: Schönbrunn; the Belvedere

EDWARD HARTWIG (ZAIKS): the Wawel Castle, Cracow

The cartouches at the head of each chapter are by Diana Bloomfield.

Each chapter is also illustrated by certain additional pictures. We are grateful to Mrs Judy Blofeld for her assistance in obtaining these extra illustrations, and to the following persons and institutions for permission to reproduce them, or for other help in connection with these particular palaces. The illustrations are identified by the number of the page on which they appear.

Introduction: p. 8 Foto Lucca Chmel, Vienna; p. 9 (Linderhof) J. Allan Cash, London; (Malmaison and Belvedere) British Museum, photos by R. B. Fleming & Co., London; (Turin) Gabinetto delle Stampe, Milan; p. 10 (the Quirinal) Edwin Smith; (Versailles) Ian Graham; (Escorial) Kerry Dundas; (Windsor Castle) Central Press Photos Ltd; p. 11 (Queluz) Kerry Dundas; (Tsarskoe Selo) Pushkin Museum

Hampton Court: All the photographs are reproduced by gracious permission of Her Majesty the Queen. p. 13 Pix Photos Ltd, photo by G. F. Allen; p. 14 Ashmolean Museum, Oxford; p. 15 (above) British Museum; (below) and p. 19 A. C. Cooper; p. 16 Aerofilms Ltd

Windsor Castle: All the photographs are reproduced by gracious permission of Her Majesty the Queen. p. 26 (St George's Chapel, Kip's engraving, Windsor in 1667), p. 28 (Holler), p. 29 (State reception) British Museum, photos by R. B. Fleming & Co; p. 26 (air view) Aerofilms Ltd; p. 29 (battle scene) A. C. Cooper

Holyroodhouse: All the photographs are reproduced by gracious permission of Her Majesty the Queen. p. 36 (Kyng of Skotts Palas, De Wet, view of Edinburgh) Edinburgh Central Public Library; p. 36 (John Knox), p. 37 (Mary, Queen of Scots) National Galleries of Scotland, photos by Annan, Glasgow; p. 37 (Chalmers) National Galleries of Scotland, photo by Tom Scott

Versailles: p. 47 (parade), p. 48 (Le Nôtre and Siamese Ambassadors) British Museum; p. 47 (J-B Martin) Giraudon, Paris; p. 48 (Louis XIV's family) The Wallace Collection, London; pp. 50–1 René-Jacques, Paris

Malmaison: p. 54 Giraudon, Paris; p. 63 (Joséphine) Laverton

Fontainebleau: p. 67 British Museum; p. 74 Giraudon, Paris

Charlottenburg: p. 80 (both), p. 82 (Churchill) Verwaltung der Staatlichen Schlösser und Gärten, Berlin; p. 82 photo by Walter Steinkopf; p. 85 Deutsche Zentrale für Fremdenverkehr, photo by Fritz Eschen

Linderhof: p. 86 photo by Peter Keetman; p. 87, p. 88 (Brening), p. 89 Verwaltung der Staatlichen Schlösser und Gärten, Museumsabteilung

Sans Souci: p. 96 (sketch), p. 97 (groundplan) Sans Souci archives; p. 97 (picture gallery), p. 98 (courtyard and colonnade) British Museum

The Quirinal: p. 103 (both) photos by André Held

The Royal Palace, Naples: p. 113 (bird's-eye view), p. 115 (church) British Museum; p. 114 (Homann), p. 115 (harbour) Museo Nazionale di San Martino, Naples

Caserta: p. 120, pp. 122–3, p. 133 Caserta archives

The Royal Palace, Turin: p. 133 (Werner and Blaer), p. 134 (cross-section) Gabinetto delle Stampe, Milan

The Alhambra: p. 140, p. 149 Gerti Deutsch; p. 142, p. 143 British Museum, photos by R. B. Fleming & Co

Aranjuez: p. 152 (de Aguirre) British Museum, photo by R. B. Fleming & Co

The Escorial: p. 156 (plan), p. 158 (engraving) British Museum, photos by R. B. Fleming & Co; p. 161 (Philip II and Charles V) Prado Museum; All the photographs on pp. 163, 164, 165 were supplied and authorised by the Patrimonio Nacional, Madrid

Sintra: p. 168 (both) British Museum, photos by R. B. Fleming & Co; p. 169 Secretariado Naçional da Informacao, Lisbon

Queluz: p. 179 (Queen Maria I) British Museum; p. 180, p. 184 (boudoir) Portuguese State Office, London

Tsarskoe Selo: p. 186 British Museum, photo by R. B. Fleming & Co; p. 187 Gerald Griffith; p. 188, p. 190 (pavilion) John Dayton; p. 189 The Mansell Collection; p. 190 (two upper pictures and monogram), p. 191 (private room, antechamber, and bedroom) Katherine McClure-Smith; p. 190 (after 1945) J. Allan Cash; p. 191, pp. 192–3 Pushkin Museum

Winter Palace: p. 194, p. 198 (both), p. 200 (both) Hermitage Museum, Leningrad; p. 195 (arch) J. Allan Cash; p. 195 (façade), p. 199 (above), p. 201 (both) Katherine McClure-Smith; p. 196 Her Majesty Queen Elizabeth II, photo by A. C. Cooper; pp. 196–7 Novosti Press Agency; p. 197 (both) British Museum, photos by R. B. Fleming & Co

The Royal Palace, Monaco: By gracious permission of His Serene Highness, the Prince of Monaco. p. 204 (both), p. 207 (Bressan) Palais de Monaco archives

Schönbrunn: p. 212 (both) Kunsthistorisches Museum, Vienna; p. 213, p. 214 (above right) Bildarchiv. d. Ost. Nationalbibliothek; p. 214 (above left) British Museum, photo by R. B. Fleming & Co; p. 215, p. 216 (both) Franz Votava, Vienna

The Belvedere: p. 225 (both Kleiners) Osterr. Galerie, Vienna; (plan) British Museum, photo by R. B. Fleming & Co

Huis ten Bosch: By gracious permission of Her Majesty, the Queen of the Netherlands. Frontispiece, p. 230, p. 231 (above) Archives of the Municipality of The Hague; p. 238, p. 239 (both La Fargues) Baroness Michiels van Verduynen; p. 238 (monogram) Her Majesty the Queen, photo by the Kunsthistorisch Instituut, Utrecht; p. 239 (punchbowl) Rijksmuseum, Amsterdam

Tullgarn: By gracious permission of His Majesty, the King of Sweden. p. 242 Försvarsstaben; p. 242 (Thersner) National Museum of Stockholm; p. 245 (antechamber) Lennart af Petersens; (writing desk) Nordiska Museet

The Royal Palace, Stockholm: By gracious permission of His Majesty, the King of Sweden. p. 248 (both), p. 257 (Rehn) National Museum, Stockholm; p. 250 (both), p. 254 (staircase) Royal Collection, Stockholm; p. 252 (below), p. 253 (chapel) Lennart af Petersens; p. 256 (both) Olaf Ekberg; p. 257 (Hårleman) Svenska Porträttaskivet, National Museum, Stockholm

Amalienborg: By gracious permission of His Majesty, the King of Denmark. p. 258 (engraving), p. 266 Det. Kongelige Bibliotek, Copenhagen; p. 261 (air view), p. 263 Keystone Press Agency Ltd; p. 261 (Le Clerc) Der Kongelige Kobberstik Samling, Copenhagen

Kronborg: p. 268 (Pufendorf) National Museum, Copenhagen; p. 270 (both) Keystone Press Agency Ltd

Corfu: p. 276 (citadel) British Museum, photo by R. B. Fleming & Co

The Wawel Castle, Cracow: p. 283, p. 284, pp. 284–5 (upper), p. 285 (loggia) ZAIKS, photo by Kolowca Stanislav, pp. 284–5 (lower) University Library, Cambridge; p. 286 (frieze), p. 287 Emil Rachwal